CANADIAN
SECURITY
INTELLIGENCE
SERVICE

CANADIAN SECURITY INTELLIGENCE SERVICE

Peter Boer

FOLK LORE PUBLISHING

© 2010 by Folklore Publishing
First printed in 2010 10 9 8 7 6 5 4 3 2 1
Printed in China

The Publisher: Folklore Publishing
Website: www.folklorepublishing.com

Library and Archives Canada Cataloguing in Publication

Boer, Peter, 1977–
    Canadian Security Intelligence Service / Peter Boer.

Includes bibliographical references.

Hard Cover ISBN 978-1-926677-66-8
Soft Cover ISBN 978-1-894864-94-7

    1. Canadian Security Intelligence Service. 2. Secret service—Canada. I. Title.

UB271.C3B633 2010   363.28'30971   C2009-907231-9

Project Director: Faye Boer
Project Editor: Kathy van Denderen
Cover Image: © Hemera Technologies

We acknowledge the support of the Alberta Foundation for the Arts for our publishing program.

We acknowledge the financial support of the Government of Canada through the Book Publishing Industry Development Program (BPIDP) for our publishing activities.

Canadian   Patrimoine
Heritage   canadien

PC: 13

To Kathy—
Always and forever…

Acknowledgements

WITHOUT THE ENDURING SUPPORT and encouragement of my publisher, this book would not have been possible. My thanks go out to Folklore Publishing for allowing me to continue telling the stories I feel are important. They also go to my mother for her nurturing nature and ability to maintain our dual relationship as mother/son and publisher/writer—home dinners are actually not that nerve-wracking. As well, they go to my editor, Kathy van Denderen, for her persistence, enlightenment and suggestions—every nuance only helps make this book the best it can possibly be.

Thanks certainly go to my wife, Kathy, for her incredible encouragement, love and support—this book is as much a product of her belief in me as it is of my own writing. And finally, they go to my son, Christopher, for his impromptu office visits while I wrote. I hope he knows how much Daddy loves him.

Contents

~∞✕∞~

Introduction

IF A NERVOUS-LOOKING, EXCESSIVELY sweaty man who has recently shaved and is wearing a Casio digital watch turns down maid service at your hotel, he might be a terrorist.

At least that's what the Canadian Security Intelligence Service (CSIS) warned first responders to look out for when hunting down potential terrorists, according to a briefing note the agency sent to all police departments in 2006. Having a tic and a freshly shorn beard might be the characteristics of an individual who is about to do something terrible, but any of the factors listed in the pamphlet could just as easily be attributed to coincidence and a nervous condition.

And that is the dilemma CSIS faces, both now and in the future—how do we protect ourselves and our country in a free society? As a result of the terrorist attacks of September 11, 2001, in the U.S., the entire continent of North America is on high alert to prevent the next domestic terrorist attack, and Canada's spy agency is right in the thick of the battle. The arrests of 18 suspects in Toronto in the spring of 2006 have proven that there is legitimate concern an attack could take place here on Canadian soil, and al-Qaeda leader Osama bin Laden's specific references to Canada as a country to be targeted have helped make the situation increasingly more real.

Publicly, CSIS and its predecessors, the RCMP Special Branch and the RCMP Security Service, have never had an enviable history when it comes to fighting back against spies, terrorists and other threats to Canada. It was the incompetence and repeated failure of the Security Service, as well as its illegal activities following the FLQ crisis in Québec, that led to the creation of our domestic security agency, but it appears that little has changed except the uniforms and the title. The agents at CSIS are not police officers—they have no powers of arrest and do not carry weapons—and they have failed to demonstrate that they are doing an effective job of protecting our interests at home. The validity of that opinion can be seen in the public record.

By its very nature, CSIS is a secretive organization and rightfully so. Protecting our nation's secrets goes hand-in-hand with protecting our country as a whole, within reason. It is likely—indeed, I am quite confident—that CSIS has done more to keep Canada safe from rogue elements, foreign spies and militant extremists than we know about. If it wasn't properly doing its job, the evidence would be public—bombs, shootings and terrorist attacks would have been occurring on our soil. To date, we have experienced no terrorist attack that can be attributed to foreign militants. There have been a few close calls, however.

The Millennium Bomber—Ahmed Ressam—was not targeting Canada when he assembled his bomb and took the Black Ball ferry MV *Coho* across the border to the state of Washington. But, had he been successful, our entire nation would have suffered— at least our reputation would have been severely diminished in the eyes of the global community and, most importantly, in those of our neighbours to the south. That the hijackers of September 11 had no connection to Canada whatsoever—despite what press-hungry lawmakers in the United States claimed immediately after the Twin Towers fell—is a blessing of both chance and robust vigilance, always the price of freedom. The cost has been felt by more than a few as CSIS works under the radar to try to protect our country, sometimes at the expense of our own citizens.

The agency was wrongly blamed for its role in the 2002 Maher Arar scandal but was tarred with the same brush as the RCMP just the same. A number of ethnic groups have complained about harassment by CSIS agents conducting repeated interviews and tapping communications, but the cost of throttling back was demonstrated back in 1985 when a group of Sikhs who lived in British Columbia were charged with blowing an Air India flight out of the sky west of Ireland, killing more than 100 Canadians on board. The investigation that followed, full of erased tapes, forgetful witnesses and unreliable sources, proved that CSIS, not a year old at the time the incident took place, had to grow up quickly. The evidence in this book seems to support the argument that the organization did not do so.

Maturity in the world of espionage involves finding and shipping out spies and terrorists. CSIS has had some success with the former, particularly in the 21st century, but it has failed with respect to the latter. There have been several rightfully celebrated arrests of foreign espionage agents who have subsequently been expelled from the country. Terrorism appears to be the agency's Achilles heel. Although granted extraordinary powers through the police and the courts to detain non-Canadian citizens thought to be national security threats and remove them from the country, the agency has failed miserably. National security certificates, which allow the government to arrest, judge and deport foreign nationals believed to be national security threats, are powerful tools and concurrently an affront to a free and democratic society.

Of the five accused terrorists who were arrested and detained on national security certificates since the turn of the 21st century, none were deported to their country of origin. The powers of CSIS were struck down by the courts but were resurrected by the Conservative government with various safeguards implemented to add some measure of protection to the accused. However, there have been no deportations. An embarrassing cycle of unreliable sources, failed polygraph tests and questionable intelligence have created a legal quagmire from which there appears no easy exit.

What should we think of the Khadr family? CSIS would have us believe its now-deceased patriarch, Ahmed, his wife, sons and daughter are all part of the extremist movement within the faith of Islam, and some of the evidence seems to bear that out. Yet CSIS' treatment of Ahmed's son, Omar, has enraged many Canadians. As a teenager, he was shot in Afghanistan then imprisoned without legal recourse in the sprawling blight on humanity that is the U.S. prison facility at Guantanamo Bay. Omar was interrogated by CSIS, which ignored his complaints of torture at the hands of his American captors. Is he a terrorist or a misguided young soul, victimized first by terrorists and then by the U.S. government? The torture and treatment he has endured are an affront to Canada's intrinsic belief in the value of human rights.

The situation surrounding Omar Khadr is particularly shameful given the emphasis Canada has placed on monitoring and disrupting groups aimed at depriving citizens of their rights in other CSIS operations. Grant Bristow, a CSIS agent, spent almost five years undercover inside a white-supremacist group that wanted nothing more than to get rid of all non-whites and non-Christians. The resulting investigation allowed CSIS to keep its activities to a minimum and to eventually break down what was becoming a powerful force on the hate group scene, the Heritage Front. Groups such as the Front take aim at our Charter of Rights and Freedoms with every venom-filled web post and Nazi salute, and CSIS stepped in to make sure the threat the group posed was minimal.

But how does CSIS fare in the world of intelligence? That is hard to judge. Sidestepping the cliché of apples and oranges, CSIS is concerned only with threats related to Canada's national security, whereas foreign intelligence services seek out moles and spies inside the halls of power in other countries. CSIS does have agents overseas, but they are tasked solely with investigating groups that might harm Canada. Does Canada need a foreign intelligence service? When you consider that we rely on our partners in the United States, Britain and Australia for much of our foreign intelligence, without contributing much in return, a case could be made for the often-suggested but never executed idea. Are we ready as a country to make that sacrifice, to send anonymous individuals into harm's way to satisfy our curiosities? The reaction to the ongoing war in Afghanistan indicates Canadians are uncomfortable when people with real names and faces die in the line of duty. The anonymity of operating as an espionage agent might be a blessing, but Canadians believe in life more than in "in-theatre threat-based assessments." And given CSIS' lack of popularity as it quietly does its business, a foreign intelligence service might make for a hard sell.

The agency is not a failure, but its missteps are public. As Canadians, we are skeptical and proud, too proud perhaps to acknowledge that what doesn't happen and what we don't know about is proof that we are safe for now.

CHAPTER ONE

A Dubious Beginning

IF ANYONE DOUBTED THAT CANADA was a target for spying by foreign intelligence agencies when the Cold War began after World War II, those doubts were all but erased courtesy of a bumbling, egotistical Soviet defector named Igor Gouzenko. The Canadian government's treatment of him in his first few days foreshadowed the seeming ineptitude with which Canada's intelligence agencies would operate well into the 21st century.

The press learned a vital lesson from Igor Gouzenko as well—don't look a gift horse in the mouth. The story began on September 5, 1945, when the 26-year-old cipher clerk who was responsible for coding and decoding documents for Soviet military intelligence at the USSR embassy in Ottawa stuffed his shirt with 109 documents that proved the Russians were spying on Canada and managed to safely escape the embassy compound. His first stop was not the RCMP or any other government branch—he went straight to the offices of the *Ottawa Journal*. The night editor at the *Journal*, faced with a sweaty man barely fluent in English with his clothes bulging with paper, decided it was better to send Gouzenko on his way than try to understand what the Russian was trying to tell him.

But the government reacted much the same way. Gouzenko's appearance at the offices of the Department of Justice stunned the staff, so much so that Justice Minister Louis St. Laurent suggested through his staff that Gouzenko merely return to the embassy and replace the documents. Gouzenko tried the *Journal* again but was rebuffed a second time. Aware of the situation, Prime Minister William Lyon Mackenzie King wrote in his diary one evening that it would be best for all concerned if Gouzenko just killed himself.

The next day, after Gouzenko spent a frightening night at home in which the Ottawa police found several Soviet diplomatic staff inside his apartment building, the government finally took action, whisking him, his wife and son away and placing them in protective custody. A Royal Commission was convened as a result of the documents in Gouzenko's possession, and it found enough evidence to support the arrests of 18 individuals alleged to be part of a Soviet spy ring in Canada, with ties to the United States as well. One was Fred Rose, a member of Parliament for the Communist Party of Canada. Eventually 11 of 18 individuals were convicted at trial and thrown in jail for various periods of incarceration. Gouzenko went on to live a high-profile life in Canada, mostly because of his own need for money and fame. He wrote books, appeared on national television shows with a bag over his head (he was convinced the KGB was still after him) and started demanding money from the press for future interviews. He became more of a thorn in the side of the Canadian authorities than anticipated, and his death from a massive heart attack in 1982 came as something of a relief.

But Gouzenko had lifted the veil of espionage in Canada for the first time since World War II, and Canada was forced to take action. The RCMP Special Branch, latter renamed the RCMP Security Service, assumed responsibility, along with its policing roles, for counter-intelligence—ferreting out spies trying to infiltrate Canada's government and military. Canada, after all, was a signatory to both NATO and NORAD, had the third-largest navy in the world after World War II and was a hotbed of military and scientific innovation solely because of its relationship with the U.S. The two countries' common and most prominent enemy was the Soviet Union, its intelligence arms in the KGB and the GRU (military intelligence) often attached to diplomatic missions overseas and intelligence units belonging to the member nations of the Warsaw Pact, such as East Germany, Poland and Czechoslovakia, among others.

Yet counter-intelligence was not something the RCMP appeared ready for. Of what few successes are known, they are minor compared to the egregious errors and slanderous campaigns launched in the name of national security. In November 1952, a young Russian "illegal" named Yevgeni Vladimirovich Brik travelled across the Atlantic Ocean to Montréal to establish himself, at the request of the KGB, as a resident of the city. He set himself up as a photographer going under the name of David Semyonovich Soboloff, but his mission was collecting intelligence throughout the city and the country from intelligence agents, then transmitting it to his superiors.

But love quickly soured Brik's disposition toward espionage as he fell hard for a military officer's wife who dallied with him but refused to leave her husband. Brik's work suffered and, following a rebuke from the Canadian KGB *rezident*, Brik decided it was time to break from the KGB. His love interest used her husband to introduce Brik to the RCMP, who immediately snapped him up, debriefed him and released him back onto the streets as a double agent, code-named Gideon. One day, after being "disciplined" in Ottawa for drunkenly calling a Montréal newspaper and claiming to be a spy, Gideon's security service handler asked James Morrison, a member of the RCMP's "Watcher" division, to drive Gideon back to Montréal.

The Watchers, maintained as part of the RCMP's counter-intelligence duties, were individuals assigned to trail potential targets. One of these was Morrison, a seemingly well-to-do agent who loved expensive suits and going to the yacht club. What no one saw was the overwhelming debt in which Morrison and his wife lived. In order to make ends meet, Morrison went so far as to steal the Service's monthly $1000 payment to Bell for allowing telephone taps. When Bell complained it didn't receive the money, Morrison was reprimanded and told to repay the money. But he'd already found a more lucrative enterprise.

The Montréal trip had put an idea into Morrison's head—he was assigned to tail Ottawa *rezident* Nikolai Ostrovsky and now had valuable information that he could offer to the Soviets in exchange for money. The Watcher Service, at its outset, had been destined to fail. It had too few agents driving too few vehicles, and the targets they tailed were versed in the basics of evasion and espionage tradecraft. They usually knew exactly where their Watchers were and did little more than stop for coffee, go to the movies or run other simple errands while being tailed. While trailing Ostrovsky, Morrison approached him and told him he had information for sale. Ostrovsky responded with interest but made Morrison wait until the evening. Later that night, on a remote Ontario road outside Aylmer, Morrison unburdened himself to Ostrovsky, who asked for the information in return for cash payments. One of the names Morrison willingly gave up was that of Gideon. Within weeks, Gideon was mysteriously recalled to the Soviet Union for "training" and never returned.

When Morrison was transferred to Manitoba as a regular RCMP officer, the cash flow stopped because he no longer had information for which the Soviets were willing to pay. He phoned his former superior and tried to convince him that the Soviets had approached him and that he could be used as a triple agent. Instead, he was arrested under the code name "Longknife" and interrogated for nine days before he finally broke. Eager to silence the entire fiasco, the RCMP charged him only with writing bad cheques, for which he received a two-year suspended sentence and a discharge from the force.

When Morrison was identified as Longknife in the 1982 book *For Services Rendered* by John Sawatzky, the public outcry in response to learning of his traitorous acts forced the government to act. At the age of 69, Morrison was charged with three counts of violating the Official Secrets Act and sentenced to 18 months in jail. He got off easy. It was later confirmed that Gideon, in return for co-operating with the KGB when he was promptly arrested after being recalled for "training" back at home, was jailed in Russia for 15 years. In the Soviet era, the common penalty for espionage was death.

Despite these debacles, one small success came for the security service in the late 1970s and early 1980s when they arrested Hugh "Hugo" Hambleton, a Canadian academic who had been spying for the Soviet Union for decades. But it was not the hard work of the RCMP Security Service agents that brought Hambleton to justice—it was a heads-up traffic stop in New York City in 1977 where a pair of NYPD officers noticed a man throwing a pipe out a car window. The pipe contained a coded message. The man in the car was Rudi Herrman, a KGB illegal operating in the United States who had spent some time in Canada. Herrman confessed after being handed over to the FBI, revealing the presence of an asset in Canada named Hugh Hambleton. The war-veteran-turned-economics professor had spent time at NATO headquarters in Paris in the late 1950s and had ferreted out classified intelligence ranging from mundane materials, such as Allied coal production, to "cosmic"-level classified documents, the most secretive of all. One document identified a list of NATO agents working in Lithuania and Estonia that the Soviets were eager to get their hands on.

After leaving NATO to obtain a PhD in economics from the London School of Economics, Hambleton again was contacted by the Soviets, first to determine if he had unburdened himself to NATO, then to encourage him to participate in fact-finding missions to countries such as Israel, Haiti and Peru, in which he expressed interest. Hambleton filed reports on Canadian military and political developments, all from open-source material. He even wrote a report on South Africa's nuclear weapons program without ever visiting the country.

The end of the line for Hambleton came with Herrman's arrest. When the RCMP Security Service were notified of his capture, it was informed of Hambleton's activities. His Québec City apartment was searched, and he was arrested and interrogated, but inevitably nothing was found to charge him with. Hambleton omitted any details of his activities while attached to NATO, and because the work he had done after his time in Paris didn't involve passing on any secret information, there was no basis under the Canadian Official Secrets Act to charge him, but his immunity extended only as far as Canada's borders.

In 1982, Hambleton boarded a flight for London, England, despite being warned he was not welcome in the country. Within a day of arriving, he was arrested and put on trial for violating the British Official Secrets Act. At the age of 60, he was found guilty and sentenced to 10 years in prison. He was transferred to Canada in 1986 to serve out the remainder of his sentence.

When the Security Service wasn't bumbling its way through the world of counter-espionage, it was busy destroying the reputations and lives of other Canadians. In 1972, the RCMP Security Service became convinced it had a mole within its ranks and set its sights firmly on Leslie James Bennett, a long-time RCMP counter-intelligence officer who had been linked to both Longknife and, before that, British traitor Kim Philby. Faced with the impossibility in the intelligence world of trying to prove a negative—that he wasn't a mole—Bennett eventually fled to Australia, his life and career a wreck and his marriage in shambles. History has since demonstrated that Bennett was not a mole and that he was unfairly investigated.

Another man who fell under suspicion for being an enemy agent was a Canadian diplomat who had served repeatedly overseas, including in the Soviet Union, in the highest of diplomatic postings. John Watkins was, for all intents and purposes, a confirmed bachelor, but that's because the only thing worse than being a Communist during the Cold War was being gay, and Watkins was. After a distinguished career throughout Eastern Europe in the 1950s, including one as charge d'affaires in the Soviet Union, Watkins, at the age of 52, was appointed Canada's ambassador to the USSR. He made two good friends, both of whom actually turned out to be KGB agents, unbeknownst to Watkins who thought the trio merely met to chat. Watkins curiously enjoyed extraordinary access to the upper elite of the Soviet Politburo. His two friends were actually inserted into his life to watch him, and it paid off big time. One of the KGB's favourite tricks for recruiting unwilling foreigners into their envelope was seizing upon an individual's weaknesses and exploiting them.

In 1955, while on a trip through Tajikistan, an associated republic of the USSR, at a collective farm Watkins met a farmer with whom he later dined and made love. On the same trip, he shared a drunken, passionate night with a poet in Uzbekistan. The KGB seized on the farmer (named Khamal, according to reports of hotel guests who had seen the two go into Watkins' hotel room) and later sent him to Moscow, where he and Watkins re-connected. As the pair explored each other's bodies in Khamal's hotel room, the KGB's cameras were watching. Watkins was presented with the photos on his last day in Moscow and asked to provide information once he returned to Canada, or at least act as an agent of influence, using his authority to advance Soviet-friendly policy. Although there was no direct evidence that Watkins ever did anything to advance the interests of the Soviet Union in Canada, a series of high-profile KGB defectors eventually named Watkins as the target of KGB homosexual blackmail. When the RCMP interviewed the defectors, they quickly launched an investigation.

The RCMP acted quickly on the information, tracking down and interrogating Watkins in Denmark where he was serving as ambassador in 1964. There was little evidence pointing to Watkins as a Soviet agent, but the fact remained that the incriminating photos had never been made public. Leslie James Bennett was appointed to confront Watkins, an ironic twist given that Bennett himself would later be accused of being a Soviet mole. Watkins was taken into custody and brought to a Montréal hotel for a fresh round of interrogation. After several days, with no hint that Watkins had ever provided the Soviets with any information, and with Watkins refusing to admit to anything beyond his sexual orientation, Bennett informed him he was planning to file a report absolving the long-time diplomat of any involvement as a Soviet spy. As Watkins reached for a cigarette, he collapsed to the ground and died.

Although his death was initially hushed up by the RCMP and was stated to have taken place at a farewell dinner, the truth that he had died in RCMP custody eventually came out 15 years later. To this date, there is no proof that Watkins ever did anything to betray Canada.

Counter-espionage, as these stories show, was not the RCMP Security Service's strength, which was unfortunate because it was the branch's primary function. While the Service was chasing down phantom spies, another crisis was brewing in Canada, one that demanded the full response of the RCMP, the Canadian Forces and the Pierre Trudeau Liberal government. It would also portend the final days of the RCMP Security Service.

CHAPTER TWO

Fires of Québec

THE RCMP SECURITY SERVICE NEVER saw it coming. all its counter-intelligence operations had been focused on foreign espionage. The idea that a threat might emerge within Canada's own borders didn't occur to the Service until it was too late. By October 1970, the province of Québec was in flames.

Under the premiership of Jean Lesage in the early 1960s, Québec's Quiet Revolution was in full swing as the traditionally Catholic, French-speaking province began to change at a societal level. Catholic doctrine was increasingly dismissed in favour of a more secular society at a time when federalism had lost its appeal. Those Québecers forever disenchanted with the prospect of being joined at the hip with Ottawa without recognition of the Québécois' distinct society began to grumble, and the seeds of sovereignty were thus planted. They believed that Québec had no place within Canada.

Some of the disaffected in the province began taking their grievances to a level never before seen in Canada. In the early 1960s, a group of individuals formed what would become Canada's first terrorist

entity, the Front de Libération du Québec (FLQ). Over
the next seven years, in successive waves, the group
rebelled against the federalist provincial governments
of its time in a violent fashion, triggering bombs
throughout the province's largest city, Montréal.
Known as an ideological left-wing nationalist and
socialist paramilitary group, the FLQ had the goal of
separating Québec from Canada by any means necessary. The rest of Canada was seen as "Anglo-Saxon
imperialists" and the Québec government as stooges
of the establishment that had to be overthrown. Influ-
enced heavily by fights for independence in Algeria,
Vietnam and Cuba, the FLQ leadership saw its own
rightful place as the warriors of a true and free Québec. Only shocking, violent action would work, they
believed.

Using a clandestine cell system in which one hand
didn't know what the other was doing, the FLQ set
out on its murderous rampage gingerly, using explosives. The first target in 1963 was a railway track on
which Prime Minister John Diefenbaker was scheduled to travel. Despite several arrests of FLQ members
for the attempted bombing, other cells sprang into
action, igniting a series of bombs across Montréal,
most of which focused on the predominantly anglophone borough of Westmount.

The first real "victims" were the mailboxes in which
the bombs were placed, but a spectre of terror reso-
nated across the country. Financed through a string of
bank robberies with dynamite stolen from military
and industrial sites, the FLQ broadened its target base.
A bomb at Montréal's Canadian Army Recruitment

Centre killed Wilfred O'Neil, a night watchman on duty. Other bombs were detonated at English-owned businesses, banks and institutions such as McGill University and Loyola College (now known as Concordia University). In 1964, one FLQ cell descended on a gun store, killing employees Leslie MacWilliams and Alfred Pinsch.

A 64-year-old worker died after an explosion at the Lagrenade shoe factory in Montréal. By 1968, with many FLQ members now behind bars, a new, more intense wave of violence started—52 bombs were detonated within a single year. The deadliest and most public attack came on February 13, 1969, when a massive bomb tore the Montréal Stock Exchange to shreds, injuring 27 people. That even Montréal's mayor, Jean Drapeau, was vulnerable, was driven home on September 28, 1969, when an explosive detonated in a toilet at his home. He was not injured.

Riots became more commonplace in Montréal. An Israeli diplomat barely escaped a kidnapping attempt. By 1970, a total of 95 explosives had been detonated throughout the city, with the FLQ taking credit for all the incidents. The group's popularity among disaffected Québecers grew, as did its confidence. What followed became the ultimate FLQ action, one that pitched the entire province into a nervous frenzy.

On the morning of October 5, 1970, members of the FLQ's Liberation cell grabbed and kidnapped James Richard Cross, the British trade commissioner, as he left his home for work. Five days later, the FLQ struck again, but this time it was the Chénier cell that took action, snatching Pierre Laporte, the provincial minister of labour and vice-premier of Québec, from a city street. Immediately prior to the kidnapping, Laporte had been in a meeting discussing the demands of the FLQ.

The group continued to whip up support for its cause, with its leaders holding public meetings. A general strike at academic institutions resulted in massive school closures. On October 15, in excess of 3000 students attended a rally to support the FLQ. The popularity of the FLQ was growing each day.

The FLQ began acting rashly. Their list of demands for freeing James Cross included the release of 23 "political prisoners" and FLQ members, $500,000 in gold, the broadcast and publication of the FLQ *Manifesto*, the publication of the name of a police informant and the promise of safe passage on an aircraft to take them and their family members to either Cuba or Algeria in the company of their lawyers.

The authorities abided by one condition, broadcasting the *Manifesto* in both English and French on all available radio and TV stations, but they received no response from the terrorists holding Cross and Laporte. With the situation in Québec rapidly deteriorating, Prime Minister Pierre Trudeau took the bold and questionable step of invoking the War Measures Act, a piece of legislation drafted during World War II that suspended all civil liberties, and sending in the army. In response to a question from a CBC journalist who asked how far he would go to end the October Crisis, Trudeau famously replied, "Just watch me."

Soldiers rushed in to guard federal and provincial institutions. The police, emboldened with new authority, rounded up anyone suspected of having anything to do with the FLQ. While some were released within hours, others were held for up to 21 days without charge. Between October 16 and December 29, 1970, the police and army arrested 453 individuals, but they charged only 18.

Invoking the War Measures Act did not save Pierre Laporte. On October 7, the Chénier cell announced that Laporte had been executed. A map to his location was discovered, and police found his body in the trunk of a car near Saint-Hubert Airport. He had been strangled with his own crucifix.

The death of Laporte had an unanticipated effect on the citizens of Québec. They were repulsed at the thought of resorting to murder. The FLQ began to decline in popularity, and in its place the voice of a slight, chain-smoking politician named René Lévesque could be heard. He denounced the FLQ for its actions and the federal government for invoking the War Measures Act. Instead, he urged those disaffected with federalism and Québec's union with Canada to follow the Parti Québécois (PQ).

"Until we receive proof [about how large the revolutionary army is] to the contrary we will believe that such a minute, numerically unimportant fraction is involved, that rushing into the enforcement of the War Measures Act was a panicky and altogether excessive reaction, especially when you think of the inordinate length of time they want to maintain this regime," Lévesque stated.

In December 1970, police finally got wind of the location of James Cross and his kidnappers. After descending on the home, the police negotiated Cross' release. The kidnappers, in return, secured a flight to Cuba where Communist leader Fidel Castro welcomed them. Four weeks later, the men responsible for Laporte's kidnapping and execution were found hiding in a Québec farmhouse. They were all tried and convicted of murder.

The crisis had faded, but in the eyes of the RCMP Security Service, the subversive threat within the Québec independence movement was still pervasive. The actions of the FLQ had caught the RCMP Security Service completely off guard and unprepared. After the last of Cross' kidnappers were flown south to the Communist paradise of Cuba and Laporte's killers had been arrested, the Service realized it still didn't have enough information about the sovereignty movement, which had become intertwined with socialist and Communist elements.

In 1971, the RCMP Security Service launched a new unit, known as G-Ops, that would conduct undercover and invasive investigations of subversive threats to Canada. The Québec wing was known as G-2. The officers in G-2 didn't just ask questions; almost from its inception, G-2 began operating in an illegal, abusive fashion, often in direct violation of the Criminal Code of Canada.

The force recruited sources within different Québec social and political movements, trying to both collect as much information as possible and interdict where necessary. Its first substantive action—and the one that ultimately led to its downfall—was hatched in October 1972. The RCMP officers of G-2 managed to goad both the Québec Police Force and the Montréal Urban Community Police Department (MUCPD) into participating in "Operation Bricole (Fix-it)," a risky, highly illegal operation. The target was a two-storey building in Montréal on St. Hubert Street that housed three elements with subversive undertones of which the RCMP knew little—the Agence de presse libre du Québec (APLQ), the Movement for the Defence of Political Prisoners of Québec (MDPPQ) and the First of May Moving Co-operative.

The men of G-2 were particularly interested in the APLQ. The tiny agency, founded in February 1971, published a weekly "newspaper" known as *Bulletin*. The newspaper's content focused primarily on work-ers' grievances, organizations fighting against the "system" in Québec and the union struggles that the mass media otherwise overlooked. The *Bulletin*, with its devotion to the working class, was causing the RCMP some worry, so much so that it began using human sources as well as the technology available at the time to learn as much as it could about the ama-teur rag. In particular, the RCMP noted the APLQ's opposition to Bill 57, which authorized the use of electronic listening devices to fight terrorism and sub-version. What the Service subsequently learned of the APLQ, ironically enough, came through planting a bug—which had to be covertly repaired once—inside a telephone at the APLQ office. The approval for the bugging operation was received on May 27, 1971, and renewed monthly.

There were small crimes of note that the RCMP Security Service picked up on in its work. It learned that both the APLQ and MDPPQ were defrauding the government. In concert with the First of May Moving Co-operative, the groups were using APLQ social insurance numbers to draw on federal youth employment grants. Of the total, $100 was given to the journalists on staff while $35 was kept by the paper. Some of these funds were embezzled, including $9000 granted by the federal government to one individual alone. Phone calls overseas were charged to the account of a federal employee. The MDPPQ was giving $1000 per month to the Legal Commune of Montréal to defend so-called political prisoners, the few people who had been arrested and actually charged as a result of the October Crisis.

But most importantly, the RCMP learned that the APLQ was in relatively constant contact with one of the FLQ members exiled to Cuba. In August 1972, Constable Robert Samson of the RCMP learned that APLQ journalist Louise Vandelac had received a letter from Jacques Cossette-Trudel, a former member of the FLQ. Cossette-Trudel's brother-in-law, Jean Bélanger, was serving as a go-between, delivering correspondence between the two. The police knew Cossette-Trudel was sending letters to Bélanger in the hopes of having them published in the French-language newspaper *Le Devoir*; they also knew that the FLQ members were working in Cuba researching Québec and Canadian issues for the Latin American news agency Prensa Latina, which had an office in Montréal.

In Samson's mind, any interaction between a terrorist working in a Communist country and a left-wing news agency back in Canada was an issue of national security. The RCMP had enough information to arrest members of the APLQ, MDPPQ and the First of May Moving Co-operative for fraud, but Samson and the rest of the officers in G-2 were afraid doing so would effectively "burn" their sources inside. The lack of information on all three groups and their interactions with Cossette-Trudel and Prensa Latina was disconcerting to Samson—he believed the force simply didn't know enough about what was going on.

The RCMP wasn't willing to go it alone, but it was loath to share the true details of the operation with police forces stationed in Québec. The ultimate truth of the matter was that Bricole was a complex yet illegal operation—no warrant was ever issued or sought. In order to persuade the Québec Police Force and the MUCPD to co-operate, the RCMP told them the operation would be used to smash a Cuban spy network. Bricole was also veiled as a counter-espionage activity with the intent of stopping an apparent prison break-out planned for the second anniversary of the October Crisis. Samson's ultimate motivation was simple—he wanted the letter Cossette-Trudel had written to Vandelac, as well as information on APLQ subscribers and MDPPQ members.

The plan in itself was relatively simple. The combined force of the RCMP, the MUCPD and the Québec Police Force would break into the building that housed all three offices, take what documents they could find, photocopy them using a copier housed in the back of a nearby cargo van, then replace everything before anyone showed up for work the next day. Any suspicion of a break-in would be blamed on a splinter group known as the Republic Militia of Québec. A human source inside the building would let the RCMP's Samson know the best time to strike.

On October 5, the combined task force began monitoring the building. The next day, their source notified them that the best time to strike would be that evening. By this time, a dozen people working in the building were under surveillance. The task force met at an MUCPD office at 9:00 PM, ready to go. Final authority to proceed should have rested with RCMP Director-General John Starnes, but there was no time to get it from him. Instead, RCMP Superintendent Donald Cobb gave Samson the go-ahead.

Shortly after midnight, five officers in a Hertz rental truck pulled up outside the building, followed by cars ferrying other agents to the scene. The infiltration team, all carrying hockey bags, promptly removed the door to the building and proceeded to grab every single piece of paper they could find. In less than 30 minutes, more than 1000 pounds of documents were seized, including whole filing cabinets. The sheer volume of material involved threw a wrench into

Bricole's plans. There was no way the men on scene could copy and return every document later that morning. Instead, the group simply took off with their haul. The only items left behind were printing equipment and money. For security reasons and to maintain secrecy, the documents were all moved to the basement of an RCMP officer's home, where a team of Mounties started sorting through all the material.

Upon discovering the theft the next morning, APLQ staff notified representatives and lawyers for all three agencies. Suspicion fell on the police because no money or anything of substantive value had been taken—just paper. That paper, however, was the lifeblood of the APLQ—their subscriber listings, clippings, resource files and correspondence were gone. Protests were filed with the authorities, but they were intercepted and discarded by the RCMP. The APLQ believed that if the police were behind the raid, all their material would be returned to them within 90 days, as mandated by law. They were wrong.

The Mounties had long since decided that none of the material would be returned. Everything was either copied, photographed or dictated to tape and later transcribed. Short of the 70 kilograms of documents deemed "too important to destroy," the rest was, in fact, destroyed.

Samson supposedly at one point lifted a letter from the pile, claiming it was the one he had sought all along—the letter penned by Cossette-Trudel—and promptly handed it over to an analyst to build a psychological profile of the FLQ member. No one had actually seen Samson find the letter or had viewed the letter itself, though.

The analysis, which was completed by November 28, 1972, revealed little of any substance. The letter, when inspected by members of the Security Service brass in Ottawa, mentioned nothing of any spy network. Yet the authenticity of the letter was never proven, and historians later alleged that the analysis was fundamentally skewed. According to the contents of the letter, Cossette-Trudel had become a devout socialist and, although he condemned his part in Cross' kidnapping, he still tried to justify it. His access to Prensa Latina, it turned out, had ceased the same month Bricole was launched.

The APLQ had $1000 in the bank and 250 subscribers. Little else was gleaned from the document haul. Both the MDPPQ and the Legal Commune of Montréal were forced out of business as a result of the raid. The only substantive action taken after the operation was a subsequent raid on an APLQ retreat in Parent, Québec. On January 23, 1973, under the auspices of the Narcotics Act, officers were actually able to make arrests based on the presence of drugs at the scene, and they also found two more letters from Cossette-Trudel, which were added to the case file. For all intents and purposes, Operation Bricole was over, and it had achieved its intended effect—the activity of all three of the targeted organizations had been irreparably disrupted.

But the men of G-2 weren't finished yet. Another nascent political party on the scene in Québec was starting to cause some concern, especially at the highest levels of government. The Parti Québécois (PQ) had emerged from the October Crisis as a stable political alternative to Québecers tired of being rained on by federalist politicians in Ottawa. Party members openly promoted their primary political goal of seeking a sovereign Québec, separated from Canada, and, once in office, were intent on pursuing that end.

The Security Service, however, was suspicious, especially given that PQ's goal of an independent Québec so closely mirrored that of the violent FLQ. In the minds of the men of G-2, the party and its diminutive leader posed a threat to the country's national security; action was required to learn more about the party and its intentions. The Service also believed that the PQ might be engaging in acts of terrorism.

What resulted was another theft, dubbed "Operation Ham," conducted on January 9, 1973, apparently with the support of Prime Minister Pierre Trudeau. The PQ stored computer tapes with information about its operations at Les Messageries Dynamiques in Montréal. The goal of Operation Ham was simple—steal the tapes, copy them and return them to the building before anyone was the wiser. First, the Service arranged for a tour of the building to familiarize themselves with its security and layout. Second, they found a civilian living in the Montréal borough of Westmount who was willing to copy the tapes. In the days prior to Operation Ham, the Security Service set up surveillance of the building, noting the frequency of police patrols in the area and the habits and rotations of the security guards. Officers then obtained a set of keys to the building and the bypass codes for the alarm system from the alarm company.

Shortly after midnight, the group of officers made their move, breaking into the building and letting themselves into the PQ office inside. The tapes were removed and shuttled to Westmount, where it took three hours to copy all of them. The tapes were then replaced, and the team left the building, their presence during the entire time completely unknown.

Operation Ham netted a large haul of information. Included in the tapes were records for 102,500 PQ members, as well as regional breakdowns of the party's financial donations. Officers didn't find any real evidence that the PQ was involved in terrorism or other subversive or illegal activities. The information was destroyed two years later.

The Security Service wasn't finished. Several other operations of questionable conduct occurred over the next two years. In one instance, G-2 learned of a meeting on a rural property that was to take place between some Québec activists and members of the Black Panthers, a violent civil rights group based in the United States intent on advancing the rights and equality of blacks. An initial scouting report of the property was disappointing; the barn where the meeting was going to be held could not be bugged. Rather than find another way to listen in on the meeting, the Security Service prevented the meeting from occurring. In a debacle that involved a broken-down truck and a stop at a nearby bar, the Service simply resorted to burning the barn down.

Another incident occurred when the men in G-2 stole a load of dynamite that they planned to plant in an activist's car to frame him for not only the theft but also the intention of committing an act of terror. The move proved unsuccessful. G-2 went on to pluck suspected FLQ sympathizers off the streets at will, threatening and interrogating them harshly; one suspect went so far as to later claim that an officer had pointed a gun to his head. Members of G-2 started files on students, unions, activists and other political parties and repeatedly infiltrated demonstrations. The tax records of the unemployed were scoured for information. In all, G-2 was now acting like its own police force, answering to nobody, with no one in any position of authority knowledgeable enough about their activities to rein them in.

And then, much like the bombs that led to the October Crisis, which had resulted in the genesis of G-2, another explosion blew the entire unit and its illegal activities wide open.

It all began with a man being rushed to hospital after being injured in an explosion on July 26, 1974. The man turned out to be Constable Robert Samson, of G-2 fame and of Operation Bricole. The explosion had been triggered by a bomb; that the explosion had taken place outside the home of one of Québec's most prolific grocery store magnates couldn't be ignored.

At first, the RCMP claimed that Samson had been injured in a car accident, but when detectives with the

MUCPD showed up to begin their investigation, the RCMP was forced to retract this fabrication. Samson tried telling them that he had been responding to an anonymous call when he found a suspicious package that had detonated in his face. The MUCPD investigators weren't buying his story, so Samson tried to cut a deal. Citing his role in Operation Bricole and membership in G-2, he tried to persuade the MUCPD that, if they simply forgot about the bombing, he would keep his mouth shut about the work with which he had been involved. The MUCPD refused.

It was eventually discovered that Samson had been the one placing the bomb, at the behest of a family in the notorious Montréal mafia who were trying to persuade the grocery magnate to "switch suppliers." Samson was brought to trial and started talking, blurting out that he had "done much worse" for the RCMP. In a couple of his statements, he alluded to the APLQ break-in but then clammed up. He received a seven-year sentence, but with his few incriminating words, he had already ignited a fire within the Québec and federal governments.

Both governments pressed the RCMP for an answer, and the police force in turn stalled. It let loose that Operation Bricole had been based on suspicions of an imminent wave of terrorist attacks and that there might also have been a financial link between Prensa Latina and the APLQ. The RCMP launched an internal inquiry, but it was repeatedly obstructed and delayed, and so it revealed very little. Three police officers, one from each of the forces that had taken part in Operation Bricole, were trotted out before the courts and charged with failing to obtain a search warrant; they pleaded guilty. Their sentence did not amount to much—conditional discharges were laid, meaning that if they kept their noses clean, they would not have criminal records.

Furious that the police would take such actions, the Québec government, under the authority of the Attorney General, asked a judge to open an inquiry into what, exactly, Operation Bricole had been. The result was the formation of the Keable Commission (sometimes referred to as the Keable Inquiry), headed by Judge Jean Keable. At its inception, the commission was tasked with investigating the specific actions of certain members of the RCMP within the province of Québec only.

But it soon became apparent that Keable was going to broaden his mandate, probing the day-to-day activities of the RCMP as a whole. This alarmed the federal government, which had begun its own Royal Commission, headed by Justice David McDonald, into the RCMP Security Service and its activities. At every turn, the police and the federal government did what it could to prevent the Keable Commission from effectively doing its job.

While details of Operation Bricole, Operation Ham, the barn-burning, the dynamite theft and the harassment of suspected activists all came to light, both the police force and the Solicitor General for Canada, Francis Fox, refused to hand over requested documentation or to testify. Fox went so far as to seek a court injunction declaring the Keable Commission unconstitutional because it was exceeding the scope of its original mandate. After a series of hearings, a Federal Court judge finally ruled in Fox's favour, shutting down the Keable Commission. The Supreme Court of Canada upheld the decision. The ball was now strictly in Ottawa's court.

The McDonald Commission heard all the same stories the Keable Inquiry had but was able to delve more deeply into the Security Service's role. Specifically, the McDonald Commission, which was ordered to report back to the Liberal Party of Canada and not Parliament, was investigating the central issue of the nation's police force breaking the law. The evidence heard already seemed to support the McDonald Commission's mandate, as well as a revelation that the Security Service had been opening mail destined for some its targets between 1970 and 1975.

When the McDonald Commission finally recessed in order to prepare its final report, it was clear that the days of the Security Service being responsible for counter-intelligence and counter-subversion were over. The question was, what would replace it?

McDonald's answer was simple—a civilian intelligence domestic agency with strict government control. Such an idea had first been floated by a civil servant as early as 1954, but the RCMP had been quick to discount it at the time and continued to do so. Now, with the enormity of the Security Service's transgressions laid out before them, Pierre Trudeau's government had little choice but to act.

On May 18, 1983, Bill C-157, dubbed "The Spy Bill," was introduced to the House of Commons. The bill would establish the Canadian Security Intelligence Service (CSIS). Of note was that the agency would be allowed to withhold information from the Solicitor General and commit illegal acts when it was deemed "reasonably necessary."

Faced with furious opposition, Bill C-157 was scrapped in favour of Bill C-9, which included all of the recommendations of the McDonald Commission so as to ensure the new agency would be as account-able as possible. On June 28, 1984, despite some oppo-sition, The Canadian Security Intelligence Service Act received royal assent, effectively birthing the new spy agency.

However, at first, few could tell the difference between CSIS and its predecessor in the RCMP, including the employees.

CHAPTER THREE

Baby Steps

WHEN CSIS, CANADA'S NEW DOMESTIC intelligence agency, was created, little actually took place to distinguish it from its predecessor. Most of the RCMP Security Service officers who had been working in an intelligence capacity up to that point simply handed in their side-arms and badges and became civilian intelligence officers, a strange move considering the findings of both the Keable and McDonald commissions. In total, the RCMP lost 1772 officers to CSIS—accounting for 95 percent of the total Security Service.

The responsibilities of the new agency were spelled out more succinctly. It was a domestic intelligence agency, responsible for assessing threats to Canada and helping to prevent them. Unlike its southern cousin the Central Intelligence Agency (CIA), CSIS was not permitted to conduct intelligence operations outside of Canada's borders. CSIS was responsible for gathering, analyzing, storing and sharing information on threats to Canada that came in the form of espionage or sabotage, foreign-influenced activities within or related to Canada, violent activities in Canada aimed at fulfilling a political objective and activities leading to or intended to destroy or overthrow the government.

In short, CSIS was responsible for tracking down spies and subversive elements within its own borders. The agency was tasked with conducting background checks and authorizing security clearances for public service employees throughout the federal government. Some exceptions were made—the legislation allowed agents to obtain intelligence from overseas if that intelligence was directly related to the security of Canada.

Agents would have no arrest powers and would not carry weapons, which explains why the former RCMP Security Service officers had to turn in their guns. CSIS' primary job was to collect and analyze intelligence, then liaise with the necessary law enforcement agencies in order to effect an official investigation and any arrests. Its powers of investigation allowed it to spy on individuals, enter their homes covertly for the purpose of either planting electronic listening devices or conducting secret searches of the contents of the residences themselves, tap phones for a period of up to one year and open mail.

All of these activities, however, required a warrant approved by a judge before the action could take place. CSIS subsequently developed three stages of investigation. Level 1 involved routine surveillance and general observation. Level 3 was the most intrusive of all, bringing all of the Service's assets, technology and tradecraft to bear, and its use required both a signed warrant and the approval of the Solicitor General, to whom CSIS reported. CSIS was also added to the list as one of the few agencies exempt from disclosing its finances.

CSIS was granted access to databases of all federal departments and agencies, as well as provincial files, allowing agents to cruise for information on hospital admissions, mental health treatments, tax returns, passports, Employment Insurance (EI) and welfare records. CSIS was permitted to work with the Communications Security Establishment (CSE). The most secretive of all government agencies, the CSE is responsible for monitoring, processing and decoding signals intelligence from outside of Canada's borders, as well as ensuring the security and safety of the country's own communications' apparatus.

The mistakes of the RCMP Security Service had demonstrated that any intelligence agency required some form of overseer. Consequently, the CSIS Act established the Security Intelligence Review Committee (SIRC). Made up of five part-time members who were granted the highest possible level of security clearance, SIRC was responsible for reviewing CSIS operations. It was also an appeal body for members of the public service who had been denied security clearance at some level. The committee would publish annual reports on CSIS' and its own activities, as well as investigate and produce reports on any instances in which CSIS was believed to be acting outside its own authority or in contravention of law.

The organizers of this new civilian, domestic agency envisioned young, suit-wearing intellectuals with a penchant for critical thought who would form the backbone of the Service as intelligence officers. What CSIS had available when it first began operations, however, was a group of grizzled RCMP Security Service veterans, far from the international political analysts its overseers had pictured. Its first director was Thomas Finn, 46, a lawyer by training who had served in the Privy Council Office (PCO). Finn was soon to learn that, as far as the agents under his control were concerned, he was an outsider.

With a budget of $115.9 million for its first year of operations, CSIS was officially proclaimed open for business on July 16, 1984. But its doors were located exactly where those of the RCMP Security Service had been prior. The agents didn't have to leave their desks. It took another year before the agency moved to its new headquarters on Wellington Street in Ottawa.

CSIS' fledgling years were wrought with examples of tunnel vision, absentmindedness and poor tradecraft. Considering its genesis in Québec's October Crisis, the agency should have been ready to function as a bilingual entity. Yet at its inception, Finn and all five deputy directors were as white Anglo-Saxon Protestant as one could be. None spoke French, whereas every other government department was mandated to provide service in both Canada's official languages. The initial candidate recruitment process included a polygraph or "lie detector" test (which SIRC had already castigated as "pseudo-science"), yet no French version of the test was available. The "spy school" established to train new recruits—the Sir

William Stephenson Academy at Camp Borden—did not offer any of its courses in French until 1988.

The number of agents at the Montréal office was consistently cut back as CSIS chose instead to focus most of its work on the "Golden Horseshoe" of southern Ontario, including Toronto. Home to massive industry and research and development that foreign spies were inevitably after, this area was where CSIS felt the majority of its assets were needed, especially since Toronto was one of the most ethnically diverse parts of the country. The Montréal office complained about the cutbacks, but no one was listening.

CSIS placed classified ads in newspapers across the country, calling for applications for civilian officers. Each candidate was subjected to an invasive and thorough screening process. As well as the polygraph mentioned earlier, interviewees were probed about their backgrounds and previous relationships, were presented with scenarios in order to deduce their capabilities for common sense and critical thinking and were subjected to a battery of psychological tests and sessions with psychologists. Nothing was off-limits. Some questions asked applicants about their sexual orientation or their sexual promiscuity. The agency was looking for anything that could make an employee vulnerable in the world of espionage.

After finishing a stint at the Sir William Stephenson Academy (named for the self-inflated father of Canadian espionage)—where they learned about international politics, espionage, terrorism, subversion, the criminal code and firearms training (though carrying weapons was not permitted)—new intelligence officers were inevitably stationed in either Ottawa or Toronto to begin with. New employees later discovered that they made significantly less money than the ex-RCMP members, who maintained the same pay grade as when they were still in the force. In CSIS' first year, none of its agents were issued business or ID cards for fear they would show them off and subsequently identify themselves as agents.

But the agents didn't need any help with that. The first few years of operations were filled with enough missteps that demonstrated CSIS was still very much an amateur organization. As recounted in the media and later complied in Richard Cleroux's book *Official Secrets*, every attempt at keeping the agency as far below the radar as possible was inevitably compromised by sloppy practices.

When the agency bought a fleet of 30 vehicles for its agents to use for business and surveillance, it kept them locked up in a fenced-off area, but they remained visible to any foreign spy who was curious to see what the new kids on the espionage block were driving. With a camera, or even just a notepad and a pen, any passerby could easily record the make, model and licence plate number of every vehicle. This oversight was driven home one day when an agent discovered that kids had written "CSIS spies" in the dust on the side of an agency car.

To counter their first mistake, CSIS started sending vehicles home with its employees, but, as patriotic as its agents were, they were opportunistic too.

Staff were soon using company vehicles to pick up dry-cleaning, drive junior to soccer or take a weekend getaway. It was agency policy to sell a vehicle when it had been driven for 100,000 kilometres and buy a new one. Eventually, this replacement project reached the point where CSIS was replacing a car every eight days. A crackdown quickly ensued to ensure the vehicles were being driven only for work purposes.

Transportation was an issue when it came to visiting agents. Officers from other intelligence agencies were often housed at the exact same hotel in Hull, just outside Ottawa. And, to get a ride, visiting agents would simply walk across the street from CSIS headquarters to the taxi stand located there. Taxi drivers, among the most observant and talkative individuals on the planet, eventually took notice. After a cab driver struck up a conversation with a visiting agent on intelligence matters, the agent promptly filed a report. Visiting agents were subsequently handled differently.

CSIS agents were painfully obvious even when they were trying to be discrete within the civil service. When the agency started mandating French-language training for all its anglophone officers, employees of other departments easily identified them as the quiet ones in the back of the classroom. Some refused to introduce themselves or explain which department they worked for. Eventually, the standard response became, "I work for SOLGEN," referring to the Solicitor General's office, which was at least partially true.

The level of amateurism was obvious to everyone exposed to the agency in its initial years. Unfortunately, little could be corrected within the next year, and that amateur start ended up costing almost 350 people their lives.

CHAPTER FOUR

Terror in the Air

IN 1984, THE COLD WAR WAS STILL raging, and counter-intelligence—the craft of spying on spies—was the dominant focus of intelligence agencies in the Western world. The upstart agency CSIS was young, inexperienced and only starting to provide any useful intelligence as it stumbled through its first steps as a new intelligence service. Roughly 90 percent of its foreign intelligence came from its partners in the United States and Great Britain. When it came to threats to Canada, a festering plague was quickly infecting a small segment of the Sikh population of British Columbia.

With 60,000 Sikhs living in the province in 1984, mostly in and surrounding Vancouver, CSIS was not able to do much with its limited resources. And given that the agency's operatives were primarily white, it's easy to see why they had such a difficult time penetrating a violent separatist movement that quickly became one of the most significant threats to Canadians.

Thousands of Sikhs had come to Canada in the early 1980s to escape what they considered unfair and inhumane conditions in their homeland of India's

Punjab region. As India grew increasingly economi-
cally prosperous, the government of Prime Minister
Indira Gandhi began centralizing its power at the
national instead of the state level. The Sikh people
were looking for more autonomy in Punjab, their
native homeland, but Gandhi wasn't willing to budge.
Citizens and police clashed frequently, and the work
stoppages and demonstrations soon devolved into
guerrilla warfare and violent clashes. Many Sikhs
were convinced the only way to truly free themselves
from India's heavy grasp was to declare Punjab an
independent nation unto itself. They had a name for
it—Khalistan.

The non-existent country even had a consulate in
Vancouver. In BC, the most well-known name in the
separatist movement was that of Talwinder Singh
Parmar, a devout Sikh, a member of the Babbar
Khalsa (Tigers of True Faith) and a militant separatist.
He was already linked to the world of terrorism, having purchased five tickets for the hijackers of the Air
India flight in 1982. Parmar was subsequently arrested
on an Interpol warrant by West Germany in 1983 at
the request of the Indian government for allegedly
murdering two police officers and a village elder back
in India.

Before CSIS came to be, the outgoing RCMP Security Service had started a file on the Sikh movement
in Vancouver and the Lower Mainland, but it was
incredibly thin, based primarily on newspaper stories
because the organization had no informants on the
inside of the movement. At most, the "Sikh desk" had

two people working on it at any given time. The
Indian government, on the other hand, was actively
watching its citizens abroad. Even as Gandhi placed
Punjab under direct rule, her government dispatched
undercover agents in the employ of its spy agency—
the Research and Analysis Wing (R&AW) of the
Cabinet Secretariat—to Canada.

Indian agents successfully tapped into and pene-
trated the separatist movement, attending inflamma-
tory speeches and rallies at temples now under the
control of the Babbar Khalsa, translating them into
English, then filing protests with the Canadian
Department of External Affairs before the department
itself knew what had been said. The R&AW established small Punjabi-language newspapers in an
attempt to destroy the reputations of militant Sikhs by
naming them as agents of the government of India.

What followed in India was one of the bloodiest
internal battles of its time. On June 1, 1984, Gandhi
ordered Operation Blue Star to commence. Indian
troops moved into Punjab, sealed off its borders and
took up positions around the Golden Temple,
a historical monument of unsurpassable beauty and
one of the most significant places of worship within
the Sikh faith. At the time Operation Blue Star
began, the temple had been occupied by Sikh
extremist Jarnail Singh Bhindranwale and his
followers and subsequently fortified with machine-
gun nests and anti-tank weapons.

On June 5, the army demanded the surrender of
the militants holed up in the temple. Only 129 came

out, but Bhindranwale was not one of them. He and the rest of his followers braced for a fight. Shortly afterwards, the army moved in but faced fierce fighting and murderous fire from within the temple. Even with artillery and armoured support, the army had trouble penetrating the defences the militants had established. Once the army did break through, the ordeal devolved into an outright bloodbath for both sides. The army had more manpower, but the Sikh militants refused to give up. The army was forced to fight for every square centimetre of the building, in the process killing hundreds of civilians, some of them youth.

When the fighting finally stopped after an entire day, the army had suffered 83 dead and 250 casualties, compared to 492 militant and civilian deaths. The temple lay in ruins, and the floors and walls were coated with blood. In the basement, the army found Bhindranwale shot to death.

The assault on the Golden Temple infuriated Sikhs both in India and across the world. One of India's holiest shrines had become a battleground and was subsequently desecrated and, for the most part, destroyed. In Vancouver on June 6, a massive crowd formed outside the Indian consulate protesting the siege, crying out for Gandhi's assassination. The wrenching outpouring of despair and rage turned into an all-out assault on the consulate as the protesters breached the consulate's gates, made their way inside, smashed photos of Gandhi and destroyed everything they could find. One group was planning to take Consul-General Jagdish Sharma hostage but did not succeed. The police intervened and broke up the riot. No charges were laid.

Five days later, 25,000 Sikhs marched through the streets of Vancouver in protest and mourning. Militants began meeting at the Ross Street Temple, where their followers had taken control, and membership in groups such as the International Sikh Youth Federation surged. And despite this obvious level of unrest, CSIS, which was just getting its feet wet in the world of domestic intelligence, did not yet consider the Sikh militant movement a threat. At the time, the agency was focused primarily on the Cold War, as well as on groups such as the Armenians, Palestinians, Libyans and Egyptian fundamentalists. The agency had few resources in the area and little direction.

On July 3, 1984, Talwinder Singh Parmar was finally released from a West German prison. Prosecutors had determined that not enough evidence was available to warrant sending him back to India. Instead, Parmar returned to BC, vowing revenge against India for the attack on the Golden Temple. The tension in British Columbia and across Canada escalated into a form of gang violence as Indian government supporters were threatened and attacked by militants. Nationwide, Parmar's supporters started dominating temples. In Winnipeg, a group attacked India's acting high commissioner during a demonstration.

Given that Prime Minister Indira Gandhi was directly responsible for the attack on the Golden

Temple, her death and the circumstances under which it took place should have offered some feeling of satisfaction within the Sikh community. On October 30, 1984, two of her bodyguards, both Sikhs, drew their weapons and shot her dead. Neither offered resistance when confronted. One was killed on the spot; the other was later hanged. Sikhs across the world, those in Canada included, celebrated openly, but their joy was short-lived. Incensed at the assassination of their prime minister at the hands of another group, many members of India's other ethnic groups went on a rampage, killing every Sikh in sight over the course of four days. In Delhi alone, mobs tore through Sikh neighbourhoods, murdering 2733 people in that city, with thousands more killed across the rest of the country.

CSIS wasn't just young at this point, it was stretched thin. Ongoing conflicts between the Turks and the Armenian minority were occupying many of the agency's resources, as were home-grown plots against cruise missile production and the ever-present threat of foreign espionage.

Although only one officer was working on the Sikh file, CSIS had seen enough in the Vancouver area that by the fall of 1984 they applied for a warrant to intercept Parmar's communications. In the warrant, CSIS stated that they believed Parmar to be a "Sikh extremist leader" and the founder of the Babbar Khalsa. Given the tight-knit nature of the Sikh community, CSIS alleged that inserting or developing a human source was "virtually impossible."

Senior members of the RCMP Security Service had already tried to interview Parmar, but he had steadfastly refused. Unfortunately, the warrant was withdrawn and wasn't re-filed until March 14, 1985, at which time it was approved. Parmar's telephone line was tapped, and by March 27, every single phone call coming in and going out of his home was being recorded.

As the tape machines rolled, CSIS listeners quickly realized they had a problem. Although Parmar conducted some of his telephone conversations in English, the bulk of them were in Punjabi, and the agency couldn't even find a translator. Between March 27 and April 9, some 83 tapes were shipped to Ottawa for translation and transcription. By the time the Vancouver regional CSIS office found a Punjabi translator, 133 tapes still needed to be translated and transcribed. To try to make up for lost time, and in part because of inexperience, transcribers resorted to merely paraphrasing the phone discussions instead of transcribing the calls verbatim. Most of the conversations were merely rendered as neat summaries, only touching on the gist of what the calls had been about.

CSIS faced a challenge in deciding what to do with the information gleaned from the tapes. One message that had been drummed into the agency and its officers from its inception was that they "were spies, not cops." That policy meant agents weren't responsible for collecting evidence and maintaining an evidentiary chain, especially if the phone conversations seemed relatively innocuous.

In the world of espionage, the most innocent conversations can turn out to be the most serious if they are spoken in some pre-arranged code, but knowing what is innocent and what is not can be relatively impossible without inside information, which was something CSIS did not have.

The biggest hint of any potentially criminal activity caught on tape was a conversation between a man named Jang Singh and Parmar, discussing a trip that "that woman's son" (referring to new Indian prime minister and the late Indira Gandhi's son Rajiv Gandhi) planned to make to the United States in June. Parmar could distinctly be heard saying, "He should not be allowed to go back." North American intelligence agencies turned their attention to Rajiv Gandhi's upcoming trip and ensuring his security. The FBI had successfully broken up a plot to assassinate a member of the Indian cabinet in May 1985 in New Orleans, but the two suspects had been able to flee to Vancouver.

With no perceived need to hang on to every single tape of every single phone call, CSIS erased the tapes once they had been supposedly transcribed. Given the translators' tendency to paraphrase conversations, this decision would come back to haunt CSIS years later.

On May 15, CSIS started placing physical surveillance on Parmar, with a large team in any number of different cars following him wherever he went. At the government's request, CSIS conducted a new threat assessment by examining the issue of Sikh militants, and the agency perceived some risk to the nation's airline, Air India. As a result, four police officers were tasked with physically guarding the airline's planes at Canadian airports to help prevent a hijacking or to intercede quickly if one occurred. No one had mentioned bombs.

Another threat assessment, issued one week earlier, had warned of the potential for violence as the one-year anniversary of the attack on the Golden Temple approached, especially with Rajiv Gandhi planning to visit the United States. A task force comprising members of the Solicitor General's office, the RCMP, CSIS and External Affairs was established to monitor levels of protection at Indian installations in Canada. On May 28, CSIS warned of an increased risk for serious violence, and the Vancouver CSIS office was told to make the issue its highest priority.

However, the team translating and transcribing the tapes of Parmar's phone conversations was still months behind, unable to provide any real-time intelligence to support the task force. On June 6, CSIS issued another high threat assessment against Indian government interests, including Air India. The assessment was based on rumours of Sikhs telling one another that it was "not a good time to fly Air India."

Two days earlier, on June 4, the surveillance team watching Parmar noted him leaving his home with a male they originally thought was his son but was in fact another man (referred to only as Mr. X and who has never been identified). The team followed as Parmar and Mr. X drove down to the ferry terminal and boarded a ferry for Vancouver Island. Upon arrival, a car met the pair and drove them to a house in Duncan. The following morning, Parmar, Mr. X and a man identified as Inderjit Singh Reyat, a mechanic working in Duncan, drove out to an isolated area and suddenly pulled over. The surveillance team continued past them so as not to be identified, then they pulled over as well. As Mr. X stood by the car on the side of the road, seemingly keeping watch, Reyat and Parmar vanished into the woods. Suddenly, a thunderous boom echoed throughout the area. One of the CSIS agents quickly made his way into the trees to try to figure out what had happened but didn't find anything and had to return to the car to resume surveillance. Parmar and Reyat emerged from the woods and returned to Duncan. Parmar continued home while Mr. X stayed overnight at Reyat's home.

CSIS filed a report of the incident, informing the RCMP of it the next day. One of the agents working surveillance claimed the sound had been similar to a gun firing, but the Mounties did not investigate because CSIS did not want its surveillance operation burned. A search revealed that Reyat did legally own a firearm, and the team surmised he might have been showing Parmar how to use a gun.

As Rajiv Gandhi's visit to the United States drew closer, the phone conversations between Parmar and his followers became increasingly more cryptic, yet not enough to warrant any special action. The U.S. Secret Service made a visit to Canada to interview Parmar ahead of Gandhi's visit. In the end, Gandhi's trip to the United States went smoothly. As it turned out, no one had any plans to do anything about him. On June 16, with Gandhi safely back in India and little in the way of evidence to support a claim that Parmar was preparing any kind of violent action, CSIS all but ended its physical surveillance, leaving only an observation post at a home nearby from which to photograph people who came and left and record the licence plate numbers of vehicles.

On the morning of June 22, 1985, Vancouver International Airport was a hub of activity as family and friends bade goodbye to loved ones catching flights to points beyond. Many people of Indian descent were there to fly home onboard Air India flights that day. Two groups of passengers were scheduled to fly to Toronto on two separate flights— Air Canada (AC) flight 136 and Canadian Pacific Airlines (CP) flight 60.

Flight 60 was heading to Toronto to connect with Air India flight 181, which would land at Mirabel Airport in Montréal, change its flight number to Air India flight 182, then continue onward to Delhi via London and Bombay. Another group out of Vancouver was scheduled to fly CP flight 003 to Tokyo, which would connect with Air India flight 301 to Bangkok.

At approximately eight that morning, a man going only by the name of M. Singh began creating a commotion at the Air Canada counter in Vancouver. Singh was arguing with an attendant, saying that he wanted to book his luggage all the way through from AC 136 to Air India 182 in Mirabel; he didn't want to have to check it in again. The attendant tried to explain that only confirmed passengers could check their luggage all the way through, and Singh wasn't confirmed. With the line-up at the counter growing, the attendant acquiesced and gave Singh what he wanted, tagging his bags appropriately and sending them off. The luggage made its way onto AC flight 136.

Mr. M. Singh never did. He had left the airport.

AC 136 and CP 60 left Vancouver International Airport within 10 minutes of one another, with CP 003 taking off at 1:15 PM for Tokyo. Not only was the Air Canada flight missing a passenger, so too was the Canadian Pacific flight bound for Tokyo. A Mr. L. Singh had paid $1200 cash for his ticket and had checked his bags through, but he never boarded the flight. The luggage wasn't removed.

AC 136 and CP 60 arrived in Toronto, where the passengers walked to catch Air India 181. All of them were frisked and had their carry-on luggage checked before boarding.

The luggage to be transferred to Air India 181 was being scanned, but the X-ray machine had stopped working. The staff decided to use a portable bomb sniffer, the use of which the RCMP had deemed "useless" six months earlier. One bag elicited a small beep, but the beep did not sound long enough to cause any concern. The bags were sent off and loaded onto the Air India Boeing 747 named *Emperor Kanishka*. The flight was delayed one hour and 41 minutes as engineers mounted a third engine onto the airframe of the aircraft for transport back to India, a common practice.

The plane landed at Mirabel Airport at 9:15 PM. As new passengers boarded the aircraft, the luggage was scanned again. This time three bags were pulled for examination by X-ray. The decision was made to keep the bags off the flight while a Mountie, notified of the incident, went looking for an Air India security representative, all of whom were occupied. By the time an Air India employee responded, flight 182 had already taken off with 307 passengers and 22 crew members. The three bags were kept overnight and put in a decompression chamber, but nothing suspicious was found.

Meanwhile, pilot Captain Hanse Singh Narendra and co-pilot Captain Satwinder Singh Bhinder were flying Air India flight 182 toward London with an estimated arrival time of 8:33 AM, Greenwich Mean Time (GMT).

On the other side of the world, CP flight 003 touched down at the New Tokyo International Airport (now Narita) at 6:20 AM GMT. A crew of baggage handlers was waiting. As the assorted suitcases and bags were being sorted beside the plane, a sudden explosion rocked the windows of the airport terminal. The blast caused an enormous crater, sending bits of plastic and debris flying everywhere. A small fire that had started was quickly extinguished, and an emergency team responded to the explosion. None of the passengers was injured, but two baggage handlers—Ideharu

Koda and Hideo Asano—were killed. Twenty-seven others airport personnel were injured.

Nearby, crews were fuelling Air India flight 301 for its trip to Bangkok, the plane to which the bags were to have been transferred. The bag in which the bomb had been transported belonged to L. Singh, who had never boarded the plane in Vancouver.

Over the Atlantic Ocean, Air India flight 182 checked in with Shanwick Control in Ireland at 7:06 AM GMT. At 7:14:01 GMT, the aircraft vanished from radar screens in the air traffic control centre. A controller contacted TWA flight 770, which was flying behind and above the Air India plane to make contact, but the TWA pilot was unsuccessful. Another aircraft in the area, CP 282, replied that it could see only the TWA plane.

Sixteen minutes later, the Irish Marine Rescue Co-ordination Centre was contacted. A general alert was issued to all vessels in the area to look for wreckage at Air India's last known location, 180 miles (290 kilometres) southwest of Cork, Ireland. At 8:29 AM, the sound of the emergency locator beacon was noted. Approximately 45 minutes later, the cargo ship *Laurentian Forest* reported seeing life rafts two miles in the distance. Moments later, it reported the sight of wreckage. At 9:37 AM, the first bodies, three of them, were found.

Only 131 bodies were recovered from the waters. In total, 165 victims were Canadian citizens, 100 were Indian and 22 American. Sixty of the passengers were children under the age of 10. A coroner's inquest convened in September 1985 found that a "violent event" occurred that caused the plane to break up in mid-air, but it was later admitted to the press that "only a bomb explains everything."

CSIS and the RCMP had suspected a bomb right from the start. Parmar had issued a statement saying he had nothing to do with the bombing. Both CSIS and the RCMP had already started collecting evidence from the bomb that detonated in Tokyo. Through detective work, the explosive was found to have been packed inside the casing of a Sanyo tuner purchased on Vancouver Island one day before the surveillance team had watched Reyat and Parmar vanish into the woods. A task force was promptly appointed, headed by the RCMP but involving CSIS. Wiretap warrants were successfully sought for Parmar, Reyat and four others.

But the investigation was quickly turning sour. A meeting between the RCMP and CSIS revealed that CSIS had only transcripts of most of the conversations that took place on Parmar's phone line. Only 54 tapes had survived, covering only the months of April and May, not the critical month of June. The agency claimed nothing incriminating was found on the tapes, which they continued to erase after the bombing took place. It was exasperating for the RCMP, but CSIS did allow the RCMP to use the transcripts to obtain warrants. It was one of the few concessions on the part of the agency in the months to come as the two sides haggled over what the RCMP could use as CSIS tried to defend its sources. The RCMP concluded that the intelligence agency was deliberately with-holding tapes and photographs taken during its sur-veillance operation on Vancouver Island when, in fact, there was nothing to hand over.

The CSIS trip to Vancouver Island particularly annoyed the RCMP because of what wasn't done immediately after the "gunshot" had been heard. Although CSIS watcher Larry Lowe had done a quick sweep and found no gun shell casings in the woods, little else was done to find out what had actually happened. No serious search of the site had been conducted, no confrontation of either Reyat or Parmar, no interviews or follow-up, and Mr. X had never been identified. Lowe was hauled in and asked to listen to an assortment of sounds, and he conceded that what he heard sounded more like dynamite than a gunshot.

A search of the wooded area ensued on June 28 with an RCMP explosives team, including a dog and handler, brought to the site. Over the course of three days, two blasting caps and a paper wrapper were found, as was a particular area of the woods where it appeared a bomb had indeed gone off.

The RCMP were now focusing in on Reyat. In can-vassing the Duncan area, they came across a friend of his, Kenneth Slade, involved in drilling, who confessed to giving Reyat 10 sticks of dynamite. The RCMP discovered that Reyat had purchased the Sanyo tuner.

It was enough for the RCMP. On November 6, 1985, the RCMP arrested the Duncan mechanic and charged him with conspiracy to commit murder, conspiracy to endanger the safety of an aircraft and possession of explosives. A search of his home turned up a receipt for the Sanyo tuner, dynamite, gunpowder and two handguns. In the end, the charges were reduced to possession of explosives and illegal possession of a firearm, for which he was fined $2000.

There was more violence to come. On May 25, 1986, Punjab cabinet minister Malkiat Singh Sidhu came to Canada on a private trip for a wedding. While travelling down an isolated logging road in BC, his vehicle was forced off the road and surrounded by a group of Sikhs. Jaspal Singh Atwal, a member of the International Sikh Youth Federation, shot Sidhu four times, one of which was in the chest. Miraculously, Sidhu survived the attack (only to be gunned down in India in April 1991 and killed).

It was another black eye for CSIS. Had they bothered to check their taps the day Sidhu was attacked instead of the day after, they would have found that part of the plot had been discussed the day before it took place. The tapes were handed over to the RCMP, who laid charges against nine militants. Unfortunately, it was later discovered that the CSIS source used to obtain the tap had fed the agency misinformation, which made the warrant illegal and the intercepts inadmissible in court. Still, four of the militants were jailed for 20 years.

Parmar and Reyat never left the RCMP's sights. On June 13, 1986, Parmar and five others were charged with plotting to bomb the Indian Parliament and kidnap the children of Indian members of Parliament.

Again the Crown's case fell into disarray—when the government refused to divulge the names of sources in an affidavit sworn in the case, the charges were withdrawn and Parmar was set free. He didn't stay in Canada for long, fleeing for Pakistan and leaving his wife and son behind. Reyat had disappeared too, fleeing to England in July 1986. The RCMP, through the British, were still pursuing a case against him.

On February 1, 1988, Reyat was arrested in England and extradited to Canada in December of the following year. He was charged with two counts of manslaughter in the Tokyo bombings, five counts of making or possessing an explosive, making an explosive device to damage property and making an explosive to assist others to cause damage to property. On May 10, 1991, Justice Raymond Paris, after hearing from 200 witnesses over seven months, found Reyat guilty on all seven charges but sent him to jail for only 10 years, stating the Crown failed to prove he had intended to harm anyone and that Reyat was "a man of remarkably good character."

There were still many unanswered questions about the Air India bombing, but neither CSIS nor the RCMP were going to get them from Reyat, who was refusing to talk. Parmar was also unavailable. On October 14, 1992, Indian police claimed they had found Parmar dead, along with five others. His death had occurred during a firefight with police, they claimed, but his body was quickly cremated. CSIS later revealed and confirmed that he had been arrested, tortured for nine days and then killed.

In scouring what intercepts it had, CSIS turned up some valuable information. It caught a conversation between Parmar and a sympathetic ticket agent on June 16, 1985. Parmar had told the ticket agent that he should, "Plan to go to India as soon as possible." The ticket agent never went.

On June 19, Parmar and an associate talked on the phone, with Parmar asking him if he had "written the story yet." A return phone call by the associate later that day records him telling Parmar he had "written the story." On the day of bombing, the associate called Parmar, who asked if he had "mail (sic) the letters."

The investigation was still a frustrating pursuit for CSIS. An internal memo written in February 1989 noted the "limited understanding of this complex subject," as well as few resources. It also explained that no "reliable human sources" were available to help in the investigation.

The RCMP, however, caught a break. After a $1 million reward was offered in 1995 for any information pertaining to the bombings, a woman came forward in 1999. Known as "Ms. D.," she began talking to the press, CSIS and the RCMP, as much seeking information about the bombing as hinting she had some evidence that might be useful.

It seemed Ms. D. had worked at a school run by Ripudaman Singh Malik, who CSIS and the RCMP suspected of bankrolling the bombings, until she had been fired. Although Ms. D. had been interviewed more than once and had told the RCMP she had never heard Malik discuss the Air India bombings, she was now saying she had confronted Malik, for whom she had professed her love, with a newspaper article that suggested he was involved. According to Ms. D., Malik confessed that he had overseen and bankrolled the entire operation at Parmar's request. It was Kamloops mill worker Ajaib Singh Bagri, she said, who had delivered the bombs to the airport.

The information provided by Ms. D. wasn't great, but it was better than what the RCMP had. Malik and Bagri were subsequently arrested and charged on October 30, 2000, with 329 counts of first-degree murder, an additional count each for the murders of the two Japanese baggage handlers and one count each of conspiracy to commit murder. Reyat was re-arrested and also charged with first-degree murder.

The ensuing trial in Vancouver became one of the most sensational and controversial in Canadian legal history. For its proceedings, a new $16-million courtroom was built. Malik and Bagri spent 30 months in pre-trial custody before the trial began. Justice Bruce Ian Josephson presided over the trial, which sat without a jury. The Crown decided to add Reyat to the witness list after reducing the charge against him to manslaughter, to which Reyat pleaded guilty and received five more years in jail.

In hindsight, it would have been in the best interests of the Crown to actually interview Reyat ahead of time to get some indication of what he might say under oath, but that never happened. As a result, Reyat took the stand and lied through his teeth, claiming among other things that Parmar had come to see him with the never-identified Mr. X about converting his vehicle to propane. (Justice Josephson later referred to Reyat as an "unmitigated liar under oath," and he was subsequently charged with perjury.)

Despite all the other witnesses called to the stand, it was the testimony of Ms. D. on whom the entire case hung, and she failed to hold up under questioning, admitting that she loved Malik, in spite of testifying against him. Despite the 19 months of trial, 230 actual trial days, 115 witnesses and a total of $140 million spent investigating the case and on the trial itself, nothing the Crown had was enough to warrant the charges against Malik and Bagri. After the trial finished in December 2004, Justice Josephson took until March 16, 2005, to announce both men not guilty.

The families of the victims were outraged, calling for an appeal, but the Crown was forced to admit there were no grounds on which to do so. Faced with growing anger among not only the families of the victims but also the rest of the Sikh community, the Liberal government of Paul Martin announced it would ask former Ontario premier Bob Rae to assess whether or not a Commission of Inquiry was necessary. Rae reported that such a commission could help answer some questions and ensure such a tragedy never happened again.

On May 1, 2006, shortly after defeating Martin in a federal election, newly minted Prime Minister Stephen Harper announced the creation of a Royal Commission of Inquiry into the Investigation of the

Bombing of Air India Flight 182 under the direction of former Supreme Court of Canada Justice John Major.

The commission, which sat until 2008, heard testimony from 200 witnesses and received 17,000 classified documents. Numerous stories of the police experiencing difficulties dealing with CSIS, including trying to get their hands on valuable information believed taped, were recounted to the retired justice. The most stunning testimony of all came from former Ontario Lieutenant-Governor James Bartleman, who was working with the Department of External Affairs at the time of the bombing and claimed to have seen a Communications Security Establishment (CSE) dispatch containing a specific, advance warning of the June 23, 1985, attack.

Bartleman claimed he had rushed the dispatch over to a testy RCMP officer who claimed he had already seen it. Consequently, Bartleman said, he never bothered following up and never mentioned it again until he was brought before the inquiry. The government countered with a slew of witnesses who all discounted Bartleman's version of events and claimed no such dispatch existed. Pierre Lacompte, a former CSE employee, stated, "Mr. Bartleman misled the families of the Air India victims and this commission. I don't know why, and I am not going challenge his integrity."

The commission has since recessed, and as of this writing is preparing its final report. According to the commission's website, Justice John Major will deliver a final report to the government sometime in 2010.

Reportedly, a 3000-page report will be issued in five volumes.

In March 2010, after an excruciating jury selection process, Reyat was brought to trial on perjury charges. On the trial's first day, the judge abruptly halted the trial and dismissed the jury after it was brought to his attention that one juror had made racist remarks. The trial is scheduled to resume in May 2010.

CHAPTER FIVE

Turf Battles

THE EARLY STAGES OF THE AIR INDIA investigation highlighted an important issue that both the RCMP and CSIS are still trying to resolve today—learning to work together. CSIS is admittedly defensive about revealing the sources of its information, and the RCMP wants to do some of the dirty work, too.

But the relationship back in 1985 outside the Air India investigation was almost unworkable. While CSIS was granted access to every single government database, both federal and provincial, the most important database it wanted access to was unobtainable. The RCMP Canadian Police Information Centre (CPIC) is, depending on who you talk to, a highly sophisticated criminal database or is a user-unfriendly piece of junk. Regardless, the information it contains is of immense value to CSIS. Every person who is stopped for any kind of offence, from speeding to first-degree murder, is contained within the system, along with corresponding notes on interviews and investigations. Especially for a spy agency like CSIS, access to CPIC would be of great help.

But the RCMP wasn't willing to share. At first, it outright refused the request to allow CSIS to use

CPIC—in fact, the day CSIS was created, the CPIC terminals in the old RCMP offices were removed. The force argued that CSIS was not law enforcement and therefore had no reason to use it. If it wanted to, CSIS could submit a written request to the RCMP. In 1985, the RCMP budged a little bit and gave the agency four terminals…that only accessed vehicle registration files, and which were all located at RCMP headquarters. Agents eventually resorted to using RCMP friends to search names for them, sneaking onto unoccupied terminals at RCMP HQ to do their own searches and at one point even stole a terminal.

In 1987, the RCMP was directed by the Solicitor General to provide more access to CPIC, and it did so, installing four more terminals linked only to the lowest levels of police files—motor vehicles and low-level counter-intelligence files, but everything else still had to be applied for in writing. It took several years before CSIS was finally granted complete access to the entire database. It was petty behaviour, but then again, CSIS could also act in an immature and unprofessional fashion. There were times that CSIS simply refused to take part in RCMP operations because the agency believed those operations were not a part of its mandate.

Some of CSIS' grievances with the RCMP date back to before its official existence. In 1983, before CSIS existed and the Security Service had been disbanded, the RCMP commissioner set up secret counter-intelligence shadow units that inevitably ended up doing many of the same things CSIS later found itself doing. These National Security Enforcement

Units drew the ire of the agency to the extent that CSIS complained to its ultimate boss, the Solicitor General. The units had 92 employees within 11 different centres. By 1988, the National Security Enforcement Units had become its own directorate.

The war between the forces was not limited just to the two entities. Ted Finn, ensconced as CSIS' first director, was responsible for watching over five deputy directors, four of whom were ex-RCMP. There was a more substantial connection between the deputy directors—all four former police officers, at some point, had worked together on Operation Featherbed, a file so secret few people actually knew what was in it. Finn had access to it, as he had during his time with the Privy Council Office, but he never discussed it. The rest of the newly hired CSIS agents quickly dubbed the four deputy directors who had worked on the operation the "Featherbed Mafia." The only substantive rumour, though never confirmed, was that Operation Featherbed might have had something to do about the extracurricular activities of politicians and bureaucrats within the government.

The Featherbed Mafia, however, were not getting along among themselves, nor was Finn able to successfully lead his deputies. Their responsibilities all seemed to overlap, which inevitably led to conflict as they continued to overrule one another on important decisions or operations. The confusion was endemic. None of the deputy directors could successfully organize any sort of substantive operation, and Finn lacked the leadership skills and experience to show them how to get the work done. Inevitably all five deputies and Finn were unceremoniously tossed three years after they were hired.

Even when handed a perfect opportunity to develop a source, and a knowledgeable source at that, CSIS came out looking like a walk-on freshman football recruit, fumbling away one golden opportunity after another. The case that best illustrates this is that of Ryszard Paszkowski. Born in Poland, Paszkowski was a welder by trade who had been recruited into the Sluzba Bezpieczenstwa (SB), or Polish secret police, after his mandatory military training. Paszkowski wasn't just a run-of-the-mill tattle-tale, however, as was so often the case with would-be informers from secret police forces in Communist countries. Because he had shown so much promise, the SB had sent him to a course taught by the KGB in Kirov, Russia, in 1976, where he was trained in terrorism, murder, bomb-making and fooling polygraph tests. Upon his return to Poland, Paszkowski was tasked with monitoring both the French and American consulates.

But in 1981, facing an uprising in the form of the birth and growth of the trade union Solidarity, national leader Wojciech Jaruzelski declared martial law, cracking down on civil liberties and imprisoning members of Solidarity and suspected sympathizers. Suspicion fell on Paszkowski, who the SB believed was helping the opposition. The agent tried to leave the country using a travel visa to get to Bulgaria but was turned back at the border. On August 25, 1982, he and a friend were able to get to Budapest, Hungary, then to board a flight bound for Warsaw. Relying on his KGB training, Paszkowski had formed a "bomb" out of red candles, tape and a battery, and he ordered the pilots to divert to Munich. He was subsequently granted asylum in West Germany but was ordered jailed for four-and-a-half years. Paszkowski lasted exactly two before manufacturing his own escape using prisoners who claimed that people on the outside could help him once he escaped.

Those people turned out to be members of the SB. Instead of jailing Paszkowski, his former bosses gave him a fake Swedish passport and several thousand dollars, ordering him to kidnap two people in France and take them to the Polish embassy. Paszkowski had other ideas, instead spending his time on the beaches of Marseilles until the money ran out. At that point, he decided it was time to head somewhere else: Canada. Travelling first to Italy, he opened up to an RCMP officer stationed at the Canadian embassy in Rome. After listening to his story, the officer told Paszkowski to go back to France and travel again to the Italian border, claiming to be an escaped Polish truck driver named Robert Fisher. Paszkowski followed his orders and spent 40 days in a refugee camp, waiting for the Canadians to show up.

When they did arrive, he was presented with a train ticket to Rome and an airline ticket to Toronto. From there he was sent to Edmonton where, under the watch of his CSIS handlers, he worked as a mechanic, learning English and entrenching himself in the community.

In May 1985, CSIS decided it was time to make a move against the Poles, telling Paszkowski to contact a university professor. Upon meeting, the professor looked at Paszkowski and said, "I bring you greetings from the Polish embassy." It was a clear sign the Poles knew exactly who "Robert Fisher" was. But CSIS persisted, ordering Paszkowski to continue meeting with the professor. The professor eventually passed on a message that asked Paszkowski to report to the Polish embassy in Ottawa.

As a seasoned intelligence operative, Paszkowski didn't think actually going to the embassy was a good idea, but CSIS was anxious to identify any SB agents working in Canada, as well as any subsequent spies. In September 1985, Paszkowski made the trip, wired for sound by CSIS. He was promptly introduced to SB Colonel Stanislaw Pikarski, who asked him if he was available for work. His skills were needed, the colonel said, to "create trouble" in other countries. Paszkowski told Pikarski he'd think about it and promptly returned to Edmonton, where his controller was waiting for him. His controller wanted Paszkowski to call Pikarski back for more information, though doing so would surely demonstrate that he was, in fact, working for the Canadians.

It was at this point that Paszkowski realized he was "working with amateurs," as he later said, who didn't know how to properly conduct a counter-espionage operation. He spent the next six months working and meeting with both Polish and CSIS handlers. CSIS' patience ran out, insisting he visit the embassy in Ottawa again to ask for more information. Paszkowski relented but found out Pikarski was no longer there. CSIS continued to instruct him to keep trying, but Paszkowski had had enough. He refused to have anything more to do with CSIS and returned to Edmonton, silently putting out the word that he was available to any other intelligence agency that wanted to use him.

Word got to everyone—Italy, CSIS, Mossad (Israel) and the CIA, all of whom eventually met to figure out what to do with Paszkowski. Meanwhile, the SB eventually made contact, ordering their agent to go to Italy and make contact with someone at the East German embassy. At CSIS' insistence, Paszkowski relented, checking in with an Italian officer when he arrived. When he checked in with the East Germans, they informed him they wanted him to place a bomb on an Air India plane in Western Europe.

On the way back to his hotel room, Paszkowski decided that it was time to finish playing this childish game. He stopped at a payphone and called Interpol anonymously, giving them his hotel room number. When he returned to his hotel, his Italian handler was waiting for him. Moments later, the police barged in, grabbing Paszkowski and sending him back to prison to complete the remainder of the jail time to which he had been sentenced in West Germany.

Upon his release, Paszkowski tried to return to Canada to live and work, but Canadian officials simply refused him clearance. Instead, Paszkowski leaked his entire story to the Canadian media, putting CSIS on the defensive. The agency was forced to admit that it had hired Paszkowski, but that tactic did not work—no one was willing to let him into the country. Instead, Paszkowski used his SB skills to doctor up passports under fake names for himself and his pregnant girlfriend. When they arrived in Edmonton, the pair was immediately arrested. CSIS was furious, having no idea what to do with this spy and his partner who was with child.

Paszkowski was eventually released from custody pending the outcome of his immigration hearing, and afterwards he and his girlfriend married. Immigration Canada finally ruled that, because of what had happened in West Germany, he was ineligible as a refugee, but that status was granted to his girlfriend. She gave birth to a son, who was considered a Canadian citizen by virtue of birth. By this time, Paszkowski's refugee status in West Germany had lapsed because he had spent too much time away from the country, and Canada was forced to accept him. He eventually became a building maintenance manager in Edmonton.

The Paszkowski case was just one example of how incredibly unprofessional and amateurish CSIS was in its early years, but it wasn't the only case. As the squabbles between CSIS and the RCMP continued, a case emerged that actually required the RCMP to overrule its intelligence cousins to avoid embarrassing the country.

The case dates back to 1968 when, on December 26, two men—Mahmoud Mohammad Issa Mohammad and Maher Suleiman, both members of the Popular Front for the Liberation of Palestine—attacked an El Al jetliner in Athens, Greece, as the plane was

preparing to take off. The pair had travelled from Bei-
rut on an Air France flight with AK-47s and grenades
hidden under their windbreakers. When the plane
laid over in Athens, neither men re-boarded, instead
rushing the El Al jetliner as it sat on the tarmac, telling everyone to get off. The two men started firing
their guns, and one even threw a grenade into one of
the engines, and tossed leaflets in the air. The attack
came to an abrupt halt when a police officer clubbed
Mohammad on the head. Suleiman was later caught
trying to escape. Only one person of the 43 travellers
and 10 crew was killed in the incident.

On March 26, 1970, Mohammad received a jail sentence of 17 years and five months for his part in the
plot. His name made headlines and his face was plas-
tered in newspapers all across the world. Yet as part
of a prisoner exchange, Mohammad was set free
only a few months after his trial, along with six other
Palestinians. The former hijacker decided to set himself up as a textiles merchant in Barcelona, then
applied to Canada to immigrate to the country, citing
that he had family in Brantford, Ontario. Shortly after
making his application, Mohammad received
a request for a meeting at the immigration offices in
Madrid. He was met in a room by a CSIS agent named
George Smith, who proceeded to interrogate him.
Mohammad admitted to the agent that he had ties to
the Popular Front for the Liberation of Palestine but
denied having anything to do with the El Al attack.

Having seen Mohammad's name on the immigration list, CSIS already had a plan in place. The agency

was interested in penetrating the Palestinian community in Canada and believed that Mohammad could serve as an informant. After Smith concluded his interrogation, he handed Mohammad a visa, telling him to contact CSIS with his flight itinerary. On February 25, 1987, Mohammad flew to Toronto. One day later, CSIS agents Roger Payne and Rick Fluke arrived at Mohammad's cousin's house, interrogated him and then fingerprinted him to prove that he was, in fact, the same Mahmoud Mohammad Issa Mohammad that had attacked an El Al plane in 1968.

Unfortunately for CSIS, it never bothered asking Mohammad if he was actually prepared to become an informant in the Palestinian community. Payne and Fluke started putting pressure on Mohammad, repeatedly making phone calls and house visits to the now 47-year-old, which he found to be exhausting.

Not one to betray his own people, Mohammad, on January 15, 1988, believed it would be best if he just left Canada. By this time, the whole story had been leaked to the press, and reporters descended on his residence. The entire affair was an embarrassment for the government—harbouring a known hijacker and allowing him entry into the country was not considered to be due diligence in the world of immigration.

CSIS, however, was determined to not let Mohammad go just yet. Before he could leave the country, Payne and Fluke showed up at Mohammad's residence and took him away in a car. Over the next three days, Mohammad was moved from hotel to hotel throughout the Ontario region, never being allowed to sleep and seldom fed, all in an attempt to wear him down. Fortunately for Mohammad, his family took quick note of his absence and called in a friend, Rashad Saleh, the past-president of the Canadian Arab Federation. Saleh hired two lawyers—Marlys Edwardh and Clayton Ruby—who promptly phoned CSIS and demanded that their client be released immediately. CSIS reluctantly gave them the location where Mohammad was stashed, and Edwardh and Ruby dashed off to meet their client.

"They had him in this hotel room when we arrived and they had been questioning him. There were about 20 guys in all, some in cars outside, some in the hotel, maybe 10 or 15 in a room next door, and four guys in the room with him. They had no warrant and he had done nothing illegal. He had not been charged with a crime," said Ruby.

Both Ruby and Edwardh noticed something that astonished them.

"CSIS was with him. But the RCMP was surrounding the joint. CSIS was inside the room but the RCMP had the room next door. I don't know why they were there. I've always viewed it as very strange. I guess they were the guards guarding the guards," Edwardh recalled.

The government of the day knew everything that was going on and decided it was best for everyone if Mohammad just left the country. The tricky part was that the government wanted it done without the knowledge or participation of CSIS and without having to resort to deportation proceedings.

Mohammad agreed to leave Canada on the condition that he could return once his family, whom he was leaving behind, became full Canadian citizens. The government agreed.

The task of spiriting the former hijacker out of the country fell to the RCMP, which acted as cautiously and covertly as it could. Mohammad was picked up and driven to the RCMP security room at Pearson Airport in Toronto in the company of Saleh. Mohammad would be accompanied on a flight to London by a young RCMP inspector named Giuliano Zaccardelli (who would one day become RCMP Commissioner). The two were issued fake tickets that would be changed once they had passed through airport security. The plan was to fly Mohammad to London, then on to Algiers, Algeria, but the original tickets showed the pair travelling to London, then Algiers and ending in Tunis, Tunisia. Mohammad was not planning on completing the third part of the trip. Under the plan, Zaccardelli would travel as far as London, then leave Mohammad to complete the journey. The government had issued Mohammad a one-week travel document that would get him to his destination.

All that was left to do was sit around and wait for their flight. As a precaution, Ruby and Edwardh arrived to check in on their client and make sure everything was going according to plan. The two walked through the airport, intent on getting to the RCMP security room, when they came across a shocking discovery—both Payne and Fluke were in the airport, trying to look as inconspicuous as possible.

The two lawyers barged into the RCMP room, demanding to know what was going on, but the RCMP was flabbergasted. The presence of Payne and Fluke confirmed Mohammad's worst fear—that the Israeli intelligence agency Mossad was trying to get to him through CSIS.

The RCMP members in the room promptly left to locate Fluke and Payne and chase them away from the airport. Meanwhile, everyone else in the room was making phone calls, trying to figure out how CSIS had found out about the flight and how they should proceed next. Mohammad suddenly declared that he would only leave if someone accompanied him all the way to Algiers. The only RCMP person available to do that was Zaccardelli, but Saleh offered to go along with them. When their flight was finally called, Mohammad emerged from the RCMP security room flanked by seven men, each wearing a fedora and dark glasses—far from inconspicuous.

Although the group didn't know it at the time, CSIS was still watching. Fluke and Payne might have been chased away, but a surveillance team was in place, and they watched the pitiful procession moving Mohammad through security. The group bypassed security and were issued their real tickets. The three men then boarded the flight.

Ten minutes after the Air Canada flight for London took off into the night sky, an anonymous individual called the media, telling them that Mohammad was being flown out of the country by the RCMP. Mohammad, Saleh and Zaccardelli (who was carrying a gun but no visa or passport) were incommunicado, but the media was able to track down members of the RCMP, as well as Edwardh and Ruby. By the time the wayward trio landed in London, an entire intelligence convention was waiting for them at the airport in the form of England's MI6 and Scotland Yard. Zaccardelli called back to Canada to check in with his superiors and discovered that the story had been broken while they were in the air. He apprised Mohammad of the situation, who was escorted by a Scotland Yard official to the Air Algérie desk, where Mohammad was told that everything was fine—the Algerians were still willing to accept him.

But within a couple of hours, the entire situation changed. The British intelligence agents had already taken the airline manager aside and spoken with him. The manager called back to Algiers to try to clarify what was happening. The answer was clear—the decision on whether or not to allow the motley trio on board was entirely up to the manager, meaning that should anything happen to the flight, it would ultimately fall on his shoulders.

The manager beckoned Mohammad into a nearby room and explained the situation, but in the end, it wasn't the manager's decision to make. After emerging from the meeting, with Mohammad explaining what had transpired, Saleh spoke up and said it was probably best if they just returned to Canada. Mohammad agreed, and the pair caught the next flight to Toronto. With more than 100 members of the media staked out at the airport awaiting Mohammad's arrival, the RCMP quietly drove a car up onto the tarmac and whisked Mohammad and Zaccardelli away.

The Security Intelligence Review Committee (SIRC) was asked to investigate the entire affair and found that CSIS did nothing to sabotage the RCMP plan.

"We found that CSIS did not slip up in the entry into Canada of Mahmoud Mohammad Issa Mohammad; someone did but it was not CSIS. Nor did it compromise his attempt to leave the country," was all SIRC had to say about the issue.

Mohammad himself was more succinct, "Just ask yourselves who wanted the plan to fail and you'll have your answer."

To this day, the media still reports on Mohammad every once in a while because of the ongoing battle over his deportation. The government has ordered him out of the country repeatedly, as recently as 2008, but the order has not been executed as a result of intricate legal manoeuvring on the part of his lawyer. A *Toronto Star* article dated June 2008 states that he is still living in Brantford and makes no mention of the CSIS–RCMP fiasco.

With both agencies tarred as incapable of performing the simplest of operations, Canadians could be forgiven if they were starting to doubt not just the relationship but the capabilities of their police force and intelligence agency. Sadly, it was not the last incident the pair of agencies would bungle.

On January 17, 1986, Canadian newspapers reported a government warning that there was real potential for a bomb attack at a Canadian airport. The articles were based on information from a man in Ottawa who told police six weeks earlier that a man from Libya had shown him a suitcase containing $80,000 and told him he was trying to find someone to put a bomb on a U.S.-bound flight from Ottawa on the weekend of January 18 and 19. Based on the threat, on January 16, the government issued a warning to travellers, increased security at the Ottawa airport and asked Canadians to stay calm.

But a conflict was already brewing between CSIS and the RCMP on the issue. Six weeks prior to the warning, the RCMP had arrested a suspect, taken him to a hotel and worked on getting a confession out of him. Although counter-terrorism investigations fell under the CSIS mandate, the RCMP never bothered to tell the agency. CSIS found out on its own, six days later. As a result, when the RCMP started investigating the bomb threat more thoroughly, CSIS refused to allow the Mounties use of its watcher service for surveillance.

No bomb went off. Although the RCMP managed to get a confession out of their suspect, no charges were laid because the circumstances of the confession made it appear as if it had been illegally extracted. Had there been a real bomb, both forces would have received the brunt of criticism if their petty infighting had become public. SIRC was aware of the feud between the agency and the RCMP, noting in its 1986–87 report a "distrust" that it believed prevented CSIS from helping out during the bomb investigation.

Beyond writing about the distrust, SIRC took no action to solve the problem, only encouraging the two sides to start playing nice.

However, there were some public developments that demonstrated the two forces were capable of working together effectively. In 1989, a Lebanese Canadian named Charles Yacoub hijacked a Greyhound bus and drove it onto the front lawn of the Parliament buildings in Ottawa. The RCMP responded with an Emergency Response Team, while CSIS scoured its files and sources for background information on Yacoub. Ultimately, the two agencies came to the conclusion that Yacoub was not likely to harm anyone, which turned out to be correct. Every single hostage on board the bus was set free, and Yacoub was subsequently arrested without any further confrontation.

The back-and-forth war between the RCMP and CSIS continued until 1989, when, after many attempts, a memorandum of understanding between both forces was finally concluded and signed. The document spelled out exactly who was responsible for what—the RCMP took on their traditional roles of law enforcement and civilian protection, whereas CSIS got what it rightly deserved—all intelligence matters. The memorandum looked good on paper. It would prove more difficult in practice.

CHAPTER SIX

Internal Bleeding

OUTSIDE OF ITS OFF-AGAIN, OFF-AGAIN relationship with the RCMP, CSIS was facing more difficulties just within its ranks. Its first director, Ted Finn, had been fired, in part because of his inability to lead and generate a cohesive, functional team. For instance, a wire-tap warrant issued against one of the suspects in the Air India bombing case had been so poorly prepared (eight errors of such magnitude as the date and the year) that the agency was forced to withdraw it. The intelligence agency was also having problems defining the focus of its activities and deciding which security issues took precedence over other threats. Based on its formation as a response to the October Crisis, CSIS did a fair amount of intelligence gathering with respect to counter-subversion—it focused on elements it believed posed a direct threat to the government of Canada.

There were matters of counter-terrorism and counter-intelligence to worry about as well, but according to SIRC, CSIS had its priorities wrong. Repeated reports issued by the overseeing body referenced concern over the agency's preoccupation with left-wing groups and protesters. One report noted the agency had files on individuals dating back some 30 years.

The agency was very active in Québec, which concerned SIRC. CSIS had recruited Marc-André Boivin, a member of the Confederation of National Trade Unions, as a paid informant. This same man had pleaded guilty to bombing four hotels in an earlier labour dispute. SIRC found that Boivin had been hired as an RCMP informant back in 1973 to monitor subversive union activities. CSIS was interested in monitoring the threat posed by Communist elements within trade unions, although there were more pressing issues it could have been monitoring. NDP member of Parliament Svend Robinson released some information to both Parliament and the public that showed CSIS was still spying predominately on peace groups and communist parties, which SIRC had already cautioned it about.

In the fall of 1987, a task force formed to examine CSIS made 34 recommendations to improve the corporate climate at the intelligence service and to create a better, more positive mindset. As a result, the counter-subversion branch of the agency was completely dissolved. An audit of the branch's files found that 95 percent of a total of 54,000 weren't worth keeping. The process for filing warrants was tightened up to prevent errors similar to those that had helped Finn to lose his job, creating the legal position of "devil's advocate" to examine and argue against every single warrant. Ex-RCMP Security Service members were offered retirement, more French-speaking personnel were hired, and the agency, long dependent on old CIA and RCMP Security Service training manuals for its staff, finally produced its own.

Despite these changes, CSIS wasn't impressing everyone yet. For example, the governments of Manitoba and

Québec refused the agency access to their provincial files on welfare, child abuse, taxes and the medical and mental health records of their citizens. That changed in Manitoba after a change in government, but Québec just wasn't willing to co-operate.

More of CSIS' errors were coming to light through the press, specifically through the Canadian Press (CP) wire service. The first leaks began in June 1988 when a CSIS investigation led to the expulsion of several Soviet diplomats found spying on industry. At the end of the month, CP followed up with a story about a brewing human resources conflict inside the intelligence service. Thirty members of the Communication Intelligence Production Unit (CIPU) had signed a letter to the head of its employee association complaining that six new jobs had been added at the Toronto office while four had been cut from Montréal, although that office was following 122 spies. Three days later, another story appeared about unprofessionalism and the seeming incompetence of CSIS in security matters.

On June 20, 1988, translator Yuri Smurov had defected from his job as a translator with the Soviet diplomatic delegation in Canada. Shortly after his defection in Montréal, he was scheduled to be flown the following week to Ottawa, arriving on June 28. Rather than go to the trouble of arranging a flight, an unnamed CSIS agent simply decided to drive Smurov himself—after all, it was only a two-hour drive—and he could claim the mileage and pick up his wife along the way. The agent made the trip with a terrified Soviet defector in his car with no police escort, just a chase car containing four unarmed CSIS agents. Had the Soviets decided they wanted to get their man back, there would have been very little anyone could have done about it.

The Service was convinced it had someone on the inside leaking information to the press, but before its own internal security division could determine who it was, the leaks stopped altogether. CSIS called in the RCMP to conduct an investigation. On August 2, 1988, the RCMP raided the desk of Radio-Canada reporter Normand Lester, as well as the offices of CP. Nothing of any substance was found in either search. Frustrated, the internal security chief decided to dispatch two agents to meet with Ottawa reporter Charlie Greenwell of CJOH-TV to try to find the leak. The agents tried to convince him that giving up the name of the mole could mean the promise of receiving more inside information in the future. As a seasoned journalist, Greenwell didn't merely refuse, he decided to embarrass CSIS for thinking such an amateur approach could possibly work. He broke the story on the evening news.

The workload at CSIS was getting heavier for all involved. In 1984, the intelligence service was tasked with performing security clearances and screening all refugees, immigrants, public sector workers and private sector employees who had access to classified information. CSIS contracted some ex-Mounties to perform the massive tasks, but the process soon became hopelessly backlogged. In some cases, the agency took more than a year to complete a security check for someone seeking clearance to the "top-secret" level.

In the outside world, CSIS continued to trip everywhere it went. In December 1988, the agency sent agents to investigate protests at the Innu community of Goose

Bay, Newfoundland. The Innu were protesting NATO low-level training flights through the area, sometimes blocking the runway to drive their point home. One CSIS agent and one RCMP officer were sent to the community to try to figure out if any "foreign influences" were at work behind the protests. The pair approached a Mennonite community leader and asked him for the names of the protest leaders, which the man flatly refused to give. Information about the investigation ended up in the hands of MP Svend Robinson, who again raised the issue publicly. The Progressive Conservative government of Brian Mulroney was trying to convince NATO to build a large air base in Goose Bay at the time of the protests, and Robinson wondered out loud if CSIS was there looking for names simply because the Innu community had embarrassed the government with their protests.

The Innu were not the only Native people CSIS spied on. In 1988, George Erasmus, the national chief of the Assembly of First Nations, one of the largest and most powerful Aboriginal groups in Canada, delivered a speech in which he stated that young Natives in Canada were becoming so disaffected and feeling so marginalized that they might resort to violence and armed terrorism. The next day, when Erasmus realized the gravity of his remarks, he called CSIS to explain what he had meant, trying to prevent a probe. CSIS responded by launching a probe.

Focusing on "Native extremism," CSIS was faced with a classic example when in June 1988 a group of Mohawk people established a blockade on the Mercier Bridge in Montréal and issued several statements, hinting that there could be violence elsewhere. The members of the

CSIS probe went to the Target Approval and Review Committee (TARC)—established to decide whether or not a specific target warranted intrusive investigative method—and asked for approval to conduct a more intensive investigation. TARC gave its approval to investigate "Native extremism" but authorized only low-level intelligence gathering such as interviews and research. No phone taps were permitted.

Unfortunately for CSIS, Svend Robinson was again in tune with what was going on, finding out about the new "investigation" at the same time he was following up on the Goose Bay protests. When he raised the issue in the House of Commons, SIRC took note and investigated CSIS for its recent conduct. The findings, published as "Report on the Innu Interview and the Native Extremism Investigation," were released in February 1990 and, as had become typical of SIRC reports, absolved CSIS of any wrongdoing. An outraged group of Parliamentarians who sat on the House of Commons Justice and Solicitor General Committee hauled SIRC before them on April 10, 1990. Although the committee took no concrete action, the members let it be known that they believed SIRC's report was both incomplete and of poor quality.

It would not be the last time SIRC's investigation of CSIS was called into question and criticized. A new crisis was brewing in one of the most socially putrid communities in Canada, with links to the United States as well as Western Europe, and, despite CSIS' best attempts, its method of dealing with the problems ended up creating more bad press for the agency.

CHAPTER SEVEN

Veil of Hate

DESPITE THE DIRECTION OF A TASK force to shut down the counter-subversion unit of CSIS in 1987, which had focused primarily on rooting out Communists and bothering law-abiding union members and peace activists, the agency still had a mandate to protect the nation from threats to its security emerging from within its own borders. The true face of terrorism and the war against it was still more than a decade away. Counter-intelligence was making up the bulk of the agency's work, but there were still groups within Canada that needed investigating. In the late 1980s, CSIS realized it lacked a true picture of the extent to which hate groups—organizations devoted to the power of white people and calling for a nation free of blacks, Jewish people or any other cultural or religious group with which they could not identify—operated in Canada.

White supremacy had long been dormant in Canada because of a number of factors. The Canadian Charter of Rights and Freedoms had focused the national conscience on equality between all people, regardless of colour, belief or gender. Canada's multicultural face contributed to a higher social belief in equality and acceptance of all persons. But mostly, the institutions of hatred, such as the Ku Klux Klan (KKK), were predominately American in nature; they had first formed in the U.S., and although they had experienced a surge of popularity in the early to mid-20th century, they began fading away as the civil rights movement took hold.

The hate groups in the U.S. still existed but lacked both the membership and direction they had known previously. They were a fractured bunch, unable to agree on their core beliefs and the extent to which action should be taken, prompting dozens upon dozens of splinter groups, some violent, some not. There was no central leadership, no one person able to unite the so-called "pure race" under one banner.

Such was the case in Canada as well in the late 1980s. Several organizations were present, predominately out west in the various chapters of the KKK as well as the Nationalist Party of Canada, but no single group had a leader able to unify its membership under one roof. That didn't mean these organizations weren't dangerous—they were. Holocaust deniers and white supremacists had spread hate literature across Canada for decades. What CSIS didn't know was just how deeply the hate vein ran in the Great White North.

Thrust into helping CSIS get a true handle on what was happening was an educated, intelligent, but pompous private investigator with a knack for getting on everyone's good side. Grant Bristow, born in Winnipeg in 1958, had inserted himself into the national security scene by virtue of his work and his connections. After graduating from a Toronto community college with a business diploma, he decided to become a private investigator, performing surveillance in Toronto, conducting background checks, probing instances of insurance fraud and vandalism and working hotel security. He had started doing under-cover work, earning the trust of his targets through his amiable nature and knowledge of body language. Bristow could make friends with almost anyone in the world just by "mirroring" them—imitating his subjects' behaviours, dress and deportment.

In 1986, through a mutual acquaintance, a diplomatic delegation from South Africa contacted Bristow and asked him if he was able to help provide security for the universally reviled apartheid state's embassy in Canada. Protesters angry at the regime that offered different rights and privileges to its white and black populations through legislation often vented their feelings outside South African embassies worldwide. The envoy hinted that Bristow might be able to help by finding out more about local agitators, videotaping demonstrations and identifying individuals most likely to cause problems.

The idea of providing security appealed to Bristow, but the thought of giving a foreign government that kind of intelligence did not. Bristow promptly reported the meeting to CSIS, which actually encouraged him to take the job, and he did. As a result of Bristow's work, CSIS furnished enough information to have one South African diplomat declared persona non grata in Canada and expelled, while barring the return of another.

The following year at a bar, through a mutual acquaintance, Bristow was introduced to a fixture in the far-right movement named Max French. Again Bristow reported the incident to CSIS, which suggested he strike up a friendship and maybe see if he could attend a meeting or two. Bristow was keen to help—too keen. CSIS received two reports of its new informant bragging to local police authorities that he was working for CSIS. After the first incident, CSIS let Bristow off with a warning. After the second, it cut ties with him altogether.

But CSIS realized it didn't really know what was going on in the far-right, white-supremacist movement and took another chance on Bristow, who this time promised to keep his lips sealed. Bristow was briefed on what was known of the players in the hate movement, and he was also given a copy of *The Turner Diaries*, a novel written by a well-known neo-Nazi physics' professor. The book told of a race war that leads to the overthrow of the United States' government, the extermination of all Jewish people and non-whites and the establishment of an Aryan order. The book was regarded as one of the bibles of the white-supremacist movement. Bristow meticulously read through it.

He was, however, unable to strike up anything remotely resembling a friendship with Max French, but Bristow was, again through a mutual friend, introduced to the Nationalist Party of Canada. The hate-spewing group masquerading as a political organization was led by Don Andrews, who already had one 1985 conviction under his belt for spreading hate. Every Saturday, Andrews would hold court at his Toronto home with his followers, known as "Androids," all seated around him to listen to his latest rant. Bristow attended one meeting and reported back to CSIS. The agency told him to keep going. Operation Governor was on.

It was easy for Bristow to not just blend in but befriend the leader of the Nationalist Party. The Androids, for the most part, were unemployed high school dropouts living off welfare, looking for some sort of acceptance and feeling of belonging in their lives. Bristow, on the other hand, was educated and relatively successful. His penchant for working under-cover was particularly useful as he began to slowly earn Andrews' trust. Bristow told the group he was an orphan, devoted to the white race. As a result of his standing in the group and his growing friendship with its leader, he was appointed head of security for the Nationalist Party. One of his first jobs was to screen new recruits, requiring them to fill out forms containing personal information, copies of which he promptly passed on to CSIS.

But Andrews wasn't the largest fish in Canada's far-right pond. In April 1989, Wolfgang Walter Droege was deported to Canada after serving four years of a 13-year sentence in the U.S. for trafficking in cocaine and possessing an illegal weapon. Having grown up in Bavaria, Droege was a devout admirer of Adolf Hitler and his World War II policies with respect to European Jewry. Droege had helped form the group the Canadian Knights of the Ku Klux Klan, which he later abandoned, and had been one of a group of 11 incredibly short-sighted individu-als—10 Canadians and one American—who had tried to invade and overthrow the native government of the Caribbean island of Dominica in 1981. The group's goal was to establish a homeland and power base for the white supremacy movement. It failed miserably. Droege and the rest had been jailed for three years in the United States.

Andrews held a party in Droege's honour when he returned to Canada, a gathering at which Bristow was present. Droege and Bristow became as close as—if not closer than—Bristow and Andrews were. Droege admitted to his new friend that he had been trafficking in drugs in the U.S. to help fund his racist activities. He was also a member of the Order, a white-supremacist group based in the United States that was involved in bank robberies, counterfeiting money and outright murder. Droege had one beef, though—Andrews. Droege considered himself a man of action, a person who wanted to fight for what he believed in rather than listen to Andrews drone on every Saturday morning.

Three months after Droege returned, the group was offered what it perceived as the opportunity of a life-time. Colonel Muammar al-Gaddafi, the leader of Libya and an international pariah, sent invitations to sympathetic groups worldwide to attend the 20th anniversary of his liberation of Tripoli. Andrews saw it as a chance to find someone serious enough to help bankroll the Nationalist Party, but he was unable to attend because of a pending court date. He asked Droege, Bristow and 17 other members of the group to make the trip in his place.

The journey got off to an ominous start as members of the Italian intelligence community detained the group and tried to dissuade them from completing their journey to Libya. But eventually the group members were released and completed the trip by boat. Their hopes for financial support, however, were dashed. A Libyan officer gave them only $1000 for their cause.

While flying back to Canada via the United States, Droege realized he was in serious trouble. Their flight from Italy to Toronto included a stopover in Chicago, and, because of his drug conviction, Droege wasn't allowed to enter the United States. When the plane landed, he simply tried staying on board, but when the pilot threatened to call the police, Droege eventually left the airplane and was promptly taken into custody, as was the rest of the group. All were subjected to a body cavity search before being questioned for several hours. Bristow was furious and scared—if he was detained, he had no way of getting out of it without blowing his cover, which he was loathe to do. Bristow was eventually released, went to a nearby hotel and called Andrews, who told him to find a lawyer for Droege and get back to Canada.

A livid Droege was deported back to Canada two days later, convinced that Andrews had deliberately set him up. It was the last straw in Droege's mind. He decided it was time to establish his own group, separate from Andrews, and asked Bristow and several others to join him. Bristow agreed, reporting the development to his handlers at CSIS.

On October 2, 1989, a member of Droege's faction officially registered the Heritage Front as the newest hate group on the block. Droege had a different approach in mind from all the others. Instead of cross-burnings and *heil*-Hitler salutes, the Heritage Front membership adopted a more press-friendly "white and proud" line. Bristow was declared the leader's right-hand man. The establishment of the Heritage Front generated plenty of press when it was first announced, but Bristow was already sharing the details with his CSIS handlers, who warned him to be careful, paid him a modest stipend and reimbursed the expenses he incurred in "the line of duty."

In September 1990, Sean Maguire, a member of Aryan Nations in the United States, called Bristow to arrange a meeting. According to Maguire, one of the group's members was working on what could be a massive ecological terror attack that involved infecting crops with a virus that would subsequently be distributed through the food chain. However, Aryan Nations was being closely watched by the authorities, so Maguire suggested the Heritage Front take over the idea and implement it.

After a meeting with Maguire and the project's designer at a bar in Windsor, Droege and Bristow left with the documents for the operation in hand. While Droege pondered whether or not it would be worth trying to sell the plan to the Libyans, Bristow handed a copy over to CSIS. Its experts came to the quick conclusion that the plan was scientifically unsound and likely wouldn't work. When Bristow got word of the revelation, he was able to encourage Droege to drop the entire idea of selling the plan or using it himself.

Bristow was starting to make plenty of friends within the far-right movement. In 1990, he had met renowned and reviled Holocaust denier Ernst Zundel, one of only a small handful of Canadians ever arrested on an immigration certificate. Zundel's beliefs were fanatical and he shared them with everyone he could in the form of a popular pamphlet entitled "Did Six Million Really Die?" At the same time he met Zundel, Bristow met British historian and Holocaust denier David Irving, who was on a visit to Canada. During Irving's visit, Bristow worked as his personal bodyguard.

Droege believed that he could trust Bristow with any kind of chore. In 1989, he had dispatched his right-hand man to Western Canada to make contact with the leaders of Aryan Nations and Aryan Resistance. Bristow returned to Ontario with a membership list and an agreement to find a way to connect the Heritage Front and other groups by computer so they could more easily communicate.

Everything Bristow learned on his trip was passed on to his CSIS handlers. So too were the day-to-day activities of himself, Droege and Zundel when they travelled to the "Fatherland" of Germany in 1991, with the intention of communing with approximately 300 other neo-Nazis in Munich. Zundel was promptly arrested by the German authorities for spreading hate literature, but Bristow and Droege managed to escape. One particular detail Bristow passed on to CSIS was that in the world of hate and white supremacy, especially in Europe, Droege was a "nobody."

After the Heritage Front was officially unveiled to the public in September 1991 at a press conference, Droege sent Bristow down to Hayden Lake, Idaho, where Richard Butler, a devout white supremacist, had 20 acres of land he used to train neo-Nazi recruits. CSIS encouraged Bristow to make the trip to see if any other Canadians were attending. Bristow learned that some Calgarians and a few individuals from BC had attended in the past, but Bristow later reported that the virulent strain of hatred that ran through Butler's compound proved to be more sickening than anything he had heard before.

It was as if this knowledge had steeled his resolve, and Bristow was able to hand over two prizes to the Canadian authorities in 1992. Droege had let the membership of the Heritage Front know that Tom Metzger and his son, John, of the ultra-violent White Aryan Resistance (WAR) were coming to Toronto to speak to the group. Unfortunately for Bristow and CSIS, Droege wouldn't tell anybody when they were arriving. After trading handshakes with the two Americans when they did come to town, Bristow was able to steal away and contact his handler, who passed the information to the Toronto police. Two hours after the rally, Bristow was driving the Metzgers through town when the police descended on his vehicle. All three men were hauled in for questioning, but a CSIS agent was present the entire time. The only difficult situation was explaining the two guns in the trunk of Bristow's car, but neither was loaded and he had a proper gun licence. In the end, the Metzgers were deported from Canada and Bristow was set free without suspicion.

The Metzger arrests led to more headlines for the Heritage Front, which had a dual effect on the group. More people were interested in joining, but a resistance movement specifically aimed at the group was forming. Two groups in particular—Klanbusters and Anti-Racist Action—were ready to battle the Heritage Front head-on. In 1993, a group of 300 anti-racists clashed with police outside a Toronto courthouse as members of the Heritage Front were being escorted inside for a hearing. Later that year, 500 anti-hate activists and 60 Heritage Front members clashed outside the city's war memorial, forcing the riot police to move in. (Both incidents were later cited as the inspiration for the Tragically Hip hit song "Bobcaygeon.")

Bristow could see the activists were starting to affect members of the Front, especially the younger members who were becoming increasingly agitated and violence-prone. They were further egged on by activists who had managed to crack the two-digit code of the Front's "Hotline" and change the outgoing message, as well as get names and numbers of people who had called in. Bristow encouraged the group to respond with a similar campaign, but it wasn't enough. Instead, with the blessing of his CSIS handler, Bristow developed the "IT" harassment campaign. An anti-racist activist would be called and informed that they were "IT" (which meant receiving harassing phone calls night and day) and would continue to be "IT" until they passed on the name and phone number of another activist. The Heritage Front members took to the idea with unrestrained glee— the key was not to outright threaten the subject of the harassment campaign. Bristow himself made a few phone calls to show the others how it was done, but his handler later suggested he refrain from such activity. One woman who was the declared "IT" endured hundreds of phone calls both at work and at home for several months and later testified to SIRC that she had reached a point where she considered actually giving in just to make it all stop.

Bristow was tip-toeing his way through some other sensitive issues. On occasion, Zundel or Droege asked him to use his skills as a private investigator to track down information on activists or prominent members of the Jewish community. After consulting with CSIS, Bristow limited his investigations to information that was available to the public, such as addresses and telephone numbers lifted from the phone book, or he would say he couldn't find anything. Bristow was asked to teach some of the members about personal security. Bristow, not wanting to be seen as teaching the white supremacists too much, kept his seminar pretty basic, telling members to get unlisted telephone numbers, use answering machines that boasted retrieval codes with more than two digits and rent a postal box to receive mail.

Throughout Bristow's entire time with the Heritage Front, CSIS repeatedly warned him never to break the law. Somehow, Bristow always managed to find a way around actually acting illegally without having to damage his cover.

But the "IT" harassment campaign worked only to a point, and some members of the Heritage Front decided it was time for bold action. A group that Bristow later dubbed "the French cruller gang" robbed a doughnut shop. Bristow passed on their whereabouts to his handler, who contacted the police. Ammunition and several weapons were found.

Droege wasn't thinking small—he and some of the other members were wondering how they could possibly advance their cause on the national stage in a legitimate fashion without making late-night phone calls or declaring their pride in the white race. In concert with co-worker Al Overfield, Droege saw a possibility in the fledgling Reform Party of Canada. Overfield developed a plan to have as many members as possible join the party so they could take over the constituency associations of 12 ridings. With Overfield's plan in place, as well as his Reform Party membership, the Heritage Front made it known to upstart Reform associations in Ontario that the Front was available to help provide security for events. On two occasions, Bristow actually ended up working as Reform leader Preston Manning's bodyguard while the rest helped out at nomination meetings. At one far-right event, Overfield set up a Reform Party membership booth.

When CSIS found out about Bristow's activities, they recommended that he stop helping out with security, but he had no choice, otherwise his cover would be blown. CSIS did not inform Manning of what was going on because it didn't want to be seen as meddling in party politics.

Not all members of the Heritage Front supported joining the Reform Party, and eventually Droege himself became disenchanted with Manning and decided to undermine the party by publicly offering it his unconditional support. When word reached the party that white supremacists had made their way onto a constituency association board and had become party members, it expelled several of them to try to help clean up its image.

Bristow, by this time, was reaching the end of his rope. He was working by day, spying by night and barely sleeping in between. When Droege was charged with aggravated assault, Bristow and CSIS were faced with a dilemma. If Droege was sent to jail—a distinct possibility—Bristow would become the de facto leader of the Heritage Front, a public relations nightmare if the situation ever saw the ink of a newspaper. Instead, Bristow and CSIS started working on his exit strategy. One day in 1994, Bristow told Droege that he was taking a new job in eastern Canada and would have to leave the group. It was a lie—Bristow wasn't going anywhere, but he needed a way out of the group. The two shook hands, and Bristow, after a thorough debriefing by CSIS, was officially free.

That freedom lasted for four months. On August 12, 1994, Bill Dunphy, a reporter with the *Toronto Sun*, called Bristow at home, requesting an urgent meeting. The two met in a parking lot where Dunphy informed Bristow that the *Sun* was going to press with a story naming Bristow as a former undercover agent within the Heritage Front. Despite Bristow's pleas for more time to get his family to safety, Dunphy stated that the story would run within 48 hours. Bristow refused to give any comment for the record and quickly returned home, contacted his CSIS handler and bundled his family and a few suitcases into a car. Bristow knew what the men he once associated with were capable of and that, once the story hit the streets, they were going to be very angry.

Bristow and his family drove to a hotel, where he checked in under a pre-arranged alias. His former handler arrived with another intelligence officer, and the pair assured the Bristows they would do everything they could to help.

Any ideas Bristow had that the story would paint him in a positive light as a hero who helped fight the far-right movement were dashed when the paper came out with the headline "Spy Unmasked: CSIS Informant 'Founding Father' of White Racist Group." The story went on to allege that Bristow hadn't just been a member of the Heritage Front but had been one of its highest ranking members and that he had funnelled money paid to him by CSIS to further the group's activities. One anonymous Front member was quoted as saying, "Grant brings the wood, he brings the kindling, he brings the match and says, 'Light it.'" Another quote branded Bristow as a "government-paid villain."

The public uproar was deafening. The thought that someone was using taxpayer dollars to fund the activities of a white-supremacist group touched a strong nerve across Canada, especially in Parliament.

SIRC announced the day after the story broke that it was launching a probe into CSIS' activities with respect to the Heritage Front, and the press was in a feeding frenzy. Preston Manning, particularly incensed at the idea that his party had not only been infiltrated by the Heritage Front but also could have been spied on by CSIS itself, demanded a full inquiry.

Bristow and his family, however, were nowhere near Ontario. The family had stayed hidden inside a three-bedroom hotel suite in Toronto for two weeks under heavy guard and supported by a crisis team consisting of doctors, psychologists and a public relations specialist. The family was then shuttled off to Jasper, Alberta, for a 10-day getaway. They were free in Jasper, but the message was clear—they couldn't return to Toronto.

CSIS furnished the family with new names and set them up in a new home in the suburban community of St. Albert, northwest of Edmonton. Now known as Nathan Black, Bristow went on to study accounting. After returning to Toronto for a funeral, his new cover wasn't enough to keep the press away. One day while leaving a physiotherapy appointment, Bristow was confronted by a *Toronto Star* reporter. The next day, details of his new life, including his new name and a picture of his wife were published in the paper. The Heritage Front added its contribution using its newest weapon in the world of propaganda, the World Wide Web. Along with his new name, pictures of a dumpy-looking Bristow were posted on white-supremacist pages, as well as pictures of his new home, the street on which it was located and the security measures that surrounded it.

It was the final hit to Bristow's family. His wife left him over the publication of her picture in the paper. The media hounded Grant Bristow/Nathan Black again, but he never spoke a word. The community of St. Albert now knew of his presence and wasn't quite sure what to make of it. Furthermore, the press was pursuing the story as far as it would go. Based on confidential documents supplied by Brian McInnis, a former communications advisor to former Solicitor General Douglas Lewis, some people began to allege that Bristow, during his time with the Heritage Front, had posed as a reporter for the *Ottawa Citizen* to collect information on members of the Canadian Jewish Congress and its affiliated groups.

The press also stated that CSIS had spied on a CBC crew preparing a documentary on racism in a particular army unit. Both the *Toronto Sun* and *Toronto Star* had the confidential documents, and the government wanted them back. McInnis later stated in an interview that he handed over the documents because he was disgusted with CSIS' behaviour. He was subsequently arrested for violating the Official Secrets Act, interrogated and then released without charge. CBC's *Fifth Estate* investigative journalism program quoted Droege and Tom Metzger as stating that not only had Bristow given Metzger money but that he had also fed him information about Jewish groups in his area.

In 1995, SIRC released its report into the accusations, entitled "The Heritage Front Affair." Critics and

Parliamentarians considered the report a complete whitewash, but it did lay out some important points. It stated that when Bristow was a member, he played only a small role in its growth. Bristow at times "tested the limits...of acceptable and appropriate behaviour," but the SIRC exonerated both him and CSIS in its conclusion. It found that Bristow had received no more than $80,000 from CSIS for seven years of work, along with being reimbursed for expenses associated with his undercover role. SIRC concluded Bristow contributed no more than $1000 to the organization in his five years with the Heritage Front, a number SIRC believed hardly justified any criticism. It also found that much of the information quoted by the media originating from members of the Heritage Front itself was concocted after Bristow's true identity was revealed. For instance, both Droege and Metzger had admitted they had made up stories about Bristow feeding Metzger information about Jewish individuals and giving Metzger money.

The report concluded there was no direct evidence CSIS had spied on the Reform Party or instructed Bristow to encourage members of the Heritage Front to join, and there was no evidence whatsoever that CSIS had spied on the CBC when it had filmed the documentary. All the report asked from CSIS was to re-examine its direction and policy when dealing with human sources.

Eventually, Grant Bristow faded away from the public eye, never once having said a word about his role in the entire affair. That all ended in 2004 when the Canadian magazine *The Walrus* published a detailed account of Bristow's version of the events. He emerged from the woodwork a little later, writing a column for the *National Post* in defence of the Canadian Human Rights Commission (CHRC), which, especially in the case of hate groups, has come under a lot of fire for being little more than a police on free speech. Bristow should know. During his time with the Heritage Front, the CHRC had ordered the Front's hate-line shut down seven separate times over the course of three years.

In 2006, veteran Conservative Party member of Parliament John Williams, representing the constituency of Edmonton–St. Albert, announced his retirement from the House of Commons. The party launched a nomination race that featured former Alberta MLA Brent Rathgeber facing off against former Progressive Conservative MP Scott Thorkelson and local Conservative organizer John Kennair. Over the course of the nomination race, while working as a reporter with the *St. Albert Gazette*, I received numerous phone calls from an unidentified supporter of Thorkelson's consistently looking to share unfavourable information about Rathgeber, Thorkelson's perceived main opponent.

In my interview with Kennair, I learned that Thorkelson had an individual known as Nathan Black working on his campaign. After several interviews with individuals associated with the nomination race, as well as personally meeting Nathan Black at the nomination meeting (which Rathgeber won over Thorkelson),

I became convinced that Nathan Black was actually Grant Bristow. A man matching Bristow's description and going by the name Nathan Black had been seen in the company of several known conservatives at a provincial Progressive Conservative Party convention in Edmonton around the same time. I attempted to contact the person I believed was Nathan Black/Grant Bristow through Scott Thorkelson after the nomination meeting, but I never received a response from the man. Tragically, Thorkelson died of a massive heart attack on May 19, 2007, at the age of 49.

CSIS had done its best to keep the entire Bristow affair secret, then executed an effective damage-control campaign that eventually allowed Bristow to disappear until he was ready to resurface. That he was able to operate for as long as he did within the Heritage Front and was also able to leave the undercover position on his own terms were a testament to CSIS' commitment to operational security.

CHAPTER EIGHT

Internal Affairs

THE AGENCY'S COMMITMENT TO security, however, was lacking in other areas of CSIS, and it led to several more embarrassing incidents for the intelligence service that saw sensitive, classified information end up in the hands of the wrong people. In 1991, the Casey affair sent CSIS scrambling, trying to recover from an incident that can only be attributed to poor common sense.

James Patrick Casey was a veteran member of the Physical Surveillance Unit (PSU), CSIS' watcher unit, tasked with conducting routine surveillance of targeted suspects. In 1991, he was working on an undercover operation and, as protocol at the time allowed, took home several files that he left in his car, parked at his residence in Loretto, Ontario. The briefcase containing the files was left inside the car overnight, and sure enough, someone broke into the car and grabbed the briefcase. When Casey awoke the next morning, he found that the briefcase containing 30 surveillance files, as well as his badge and bodypack recorder, was gone.

⋘✦⋙

Jesse Barnes wasn't just a petty criminal on the outside. He had a reputation for conducting illegal business
on the inside of the prison system as well. His career
began with an on-again, off-again six-year sentence for
a series of thefts throughout Ontario. During his time
in custody, he made some important connections at
the Kingston Penitentiary. Several members of the
Montréal mafia were also serving time. Over the course
of his sentence, Barnes had befriended Vincenzo (Vic)
"The Egg" Cotroni, serving time for extortion. When
Barnes was transferred to a different institution at
Collins Bay, Cotroni gave him a letter of introduction
that Barnes presented to Benedetto Zizzo, another
member of the mob serving time for smuggling heroin.
Benedetto, in turn, introduced Barnes to several other
members of the mob family.

Barnes was released from custody in October 1978
but promptly returned in December for stealing from
several stores. He managed to escape the following
April, but his illegal freedom came to an abrupt end
only one month later when he was arrested. He was
sent to Joyceville where, with the encouragement of
his friends, he set up several illegal schemes for
inmates, including bookmaking, dealing in prescrip-
tion drugs and using physical force to collect on out-
standing mob debts inside prison. In one case, an
inmate requested a $400 loan so that he could have
some cash for his upcoming three-day "unescorted
temporary absence." Instead of returning after three
days, the inmate bolted for freedom. He was eventually caught and returned to Joyceville, but the money

was gone. In response, Barnes attacked him with a pair of scissors during an inmate movie night.

When he was finally released, Barnes decided his contacts could help him make some headway with the Ontario Provincial Police (OPP), especially given the mob's most recent request of him—killing an informant. He walked into the station and made known his acquaintances. During a two-day interrogation, the police agreed to furnish Barnes with a new identity under the witness protection program in exchange for his help. The deal was short-lived. The OPP changed its mind. Several years later, in 1992, Barnes was briefly considered a suspect in the murder of mob informant Ignazio Drago. He agreed to help the police, and charges were never laid.

But Barnes was already on the CSIS radar. In 1991, the career criminal was hanging out with some mob-related friends in Toronto at a local haunt when a man known to everyone there as a CSIS employee dropped by looking to buy $400 worth of heroin for his own personal use. The agent asked Barnes to retrieve a briefcase from the back of his car. The briefcase, as it turned out, belonged to James Patrick Casey and was brimming with field notes and surveillance data, all of which was deemed particularly sensitive and classified. The agent suggested Barnes could sell the information to the individuals under surveillance or use them as blackmail. He agreed to leave the briefcase with Barnes for one day so that Barnes could make photocopies of the information. After Barnes consulted with mob friend Wes Demarco, copies were made and the briefcase was taken to a home under renovations and hidden behind a sheet of drywall. Barnes held onto one item—Casey's CSIS identification card, doctoring it to replace Casey's photo with his own.

Barnes was feeling a little bit nervous about what had just transpired and phoned a former mob informant and handler named Sam Lo Stracco. Lo Stracco made a few calls and confirmed that CSIS was freaking out about a stolen briefcase, bringing all of its assets to bear to determine just how sensitive the stolen information was. The two arranged to meet at York Finch General Hospital, where Lo Stracco arrived in the company of an RCMP officer. Barnes opened up and told the two about the entire affair. Barnes was promptly asked to retrieve the briefcase and return with it, which he agreed to do. On his way back to Toronto, Barnes was pulled over for driving with stolen licence plates and promptly hauled off to Newmarket Station. He contacted Lo Stracco from the police station and was released shortly afterward.

Knowing through his old sources that he was now being watched by CSIS, Lo Stracco hatched a more intricate exchange for the briefcase. Upon meeting at the hospital, Lo Stracco told Barnes to go the bathroom. Once Barnes was inside, Lo Stracco joined him in the bathroom and gave him a key to a motel room. Barnes headed straight for the motel. Lo Stracco and the RCMP officer arrived an hour later, having taken a circuitous route to the motel in order to shake off their CSIS tails. Once inside the motel, the pair handed Barnes $2500 and gave him a cover story—if anyone asked, he would say he found the briefcase in a car he was driving for a used car dealer that was to be purchased at auction. The briefcase was eventually returned to CSIS.

It came to light that Casey hadn't reported the briefcase missing for three whole days. Somehow he managed to keep his job, although the sensitive information inside his briefcase had briefly fallen into the hands of the mafia.

It would not be the last embarrassing instance of classified materials ending up in the wrong hands. In 1999, a CSIS intelligence officer was given permission to take a bundle of classified documents on vacation to study for an upcoming job promotion. One evening in October of that year, the officer decided to take in a Toronto Maple Leaf's hockey game at the Air Canada Centre in Toronto. She left her briefcase, which contained one of the documents, inside her van; it was subsequently broken into and the briefcase was stolen. The empty briefcase was later found in a dumpster in downtown Toronto.

Although CSIS would not release any information about what was contained within the document, intelligence experts at the time believed it to be operational planning information. The woman was immediately fired from CSIS. The document later turned up in the hands of three drug addicts. The press found out about the incident before SIRC did because CSIS director Ward Elcock simply decided not tell the overseer body what had happened.

Both breaches were embarrassing and potentially detrimental to the Service and to the security of Canada. Unfortunately, they exemplified the cavalier attitude with which some agents and contractors approached their work with the agency.

One of the most controversial operations in the history of CSIS—Operation Vulva—was fraught with ineptitude and sloppy work. No one knows if the name of the operation was spat out by a computer or jokingly suggested by an actual person, but it did bear some symbolism to the activities that took place under its mandate.

Starting in the 1980s, "Operation Vulva" was the code name for the intelligence agency's secret mail-opening program. The secrecy around Vulva was revealed in 2002 when author Andrew Mitrovica, with the help of former CSIS agent Joseph Farrell, wrote *Covert Entry: Spies, Lies and Crimes Inside Canada's Secret Service*. Farrell, it turned out, had been heavily involved in Operation Vulva before graduating on to more important work with one of CSIS' most secretive department—the Special Operations Service (SOS), the group of men and women who actually execute operations in the field.

The essence of Operation Vulva was opening mail, which the RCMP Security Service had admitted doing since the 1950s. Under federal law, opening addressed mail intended for someone else is a criminal offence. But CSIS, as part of its strategy to protect Canada's national security, was permitted under specific circumstances to open the mail of designated target, as approved by the Target Approval and Review Committee (TARC). A federal warrant signed by a judge was required. The requirements of the warrant stated that any mail intercepted by CSIS had to be returned to the mail stream within 72 hours, both to ensure the individuals received their mail and to not arouse suspicion because known packages and letters were excessively late in arriving.

There were varying degrees of just how far, depending on the warrant and level of intrusive action permitted, the agency could go in opening a target's mail. In some cases, CSIS operatives working exclusively for Operation Vulva simply photocopied the exterior of an envelope and returned it to the mail stream. In other instances, warrants authorized agents to actually open letters and packages, but it had to be done in such a way so as not to arouse suspicion on the part of the target. Once the contents were freed, they were photocopied, replaced and sent back to Canada Post, which was in the dark about this particular side of CSIS' work.

Increasingly, recipients deemed worthy targets were found to be resorting to tiny but effective tricks that told them whether or not their mail had been opened—one could use a strip of Scotch tape to affix a hair to the envelope or include some sort of code on the exterior. The absence of any of these indicators would reveal that a particular letter or package had been intercepted and opened. Every envelope designated for opening had to be scrutinized closely. Any suspected of containing a warning "tell" were sent to Ottawa for processing and examination.

The process was not without its problems, notably because the agents assigned to intercept and convey mail were not fully trained CSIS operatives. Some adhered to the age-old rule of "work expanding to fit the time allotted," spending most of their day driving aimlessly and charging CSIS for the mileage when they only had one or two packages of mail to pick up. In other cases, the intercept mail was treated in an insecure fashion. Farrell noted some examples, including envelopes or their contents being stained with food, shredded by the family dog or accidentally opened when they were not supposed to be.

In one case, when CSIS applied the talents of Operation Vulva to its covert monitoring of the far-right movement, a critical mistake tipped off Wolfgang Droege, head of the Heritage Front, that something was amiss. CSIS had permission to conduct a fully intrusive investigation that included phone taps, covert home entry and mail opening, but it applied only to Droege. CSIS also tried to access the mail for Max French, a far-right associate of Droege who lived in the same building, but it could not obtain a warrant. The agency believed that Droege was using French's apartment to make phone calls and wanted copies of French's phone bills to determine who Droege was calling. The order to intercept French's mail, however, was done without a judicially authorized warrant. On one occasion, the agent responsible for returning Droege's mail to the stream accidentally dropped his home mail in the postal box belonging to the Heritage Front. A subsequent recorded phone tap revealed that Droege believed his mail was being tampered with.

CSIS also intercepted Holocaust denier Ernst Zundel's mail that contained the entire membership list of the Heritage Front, as well as letters of support from across the world, from professionals to prisoners. At one point in 1985, however, the workers in Operation Vulva were ordered to stop opening any packages bound for Zundel's house—luckily for them, it would turn out. In May 1985, a package arrived at Zundel's door that made him suspicious. He decided to take it to the police, who found a powerful pipe bomb filled with nails inside that, if detonated, would have killed or seriously injured anyone within a 90-metre radius. The police safely detonated the bomb, which was later linked to an anarchist group known as the Militant Direct Action Task Force, an anti-racist, anti-fascist group opposed to the Heritage Front.

Shortly after the Heritage Front became public, Operation Vulva was temporarily shut down. The focus of CSIS was shifting as, with the demise of the Soviet Union in 1991 and the rise of China as a global superpower, espionage was taking on a new face. Terrorism was becoming a pre-eminent concern, as was the possibility that Russia and China were buying up interests in Canadian business to both acquire nascent technologies and influence government direction.

According to *Covert Entry*, the role Farrell played became critical in some of the agency's biggest spy hauls in the early to mid-1990s. Farrell was moved from intercepting mail to working with SOS. The highly trained operatives in this group were responsible primarily for covert break-ins of high-value targets, often to install bugs. The team had the ability to fabricate keys for any kind of lock. Once inside, agents first videotaped the contents of the home or office before the search and later reviewed the tape to ensure that anything moved out of place during the search was put back exactly where it had been so as not to alert the target. Farrell and the rest of the SOS team factored heavily into one of the agency's most celebrated achievements—Operation Stanley Cup.

A pair of "Canadians" named Ian and Laurie Lambert had somehow come to the attention of CSIS in 1994. The couple lived in Toronto, just off Yonge Street in a 10-storey apartment building. Ian worked as a photo developer for Black's Photography while Laurie was a clerk at a life insurance company.

In reality, the two were Russian illegals, agents of the SVR—the Russian foreign intelligence agency that had replaced the KGB. Their real names were Yelena Olshevskaya and Dmitriy Olshevsky. CSIS believed the pair was operating in conjunction with a Russian officer at the Ottawa embassy. The Communications Security Establishment (CSE) obtained intercepts that showed the two used a short-wave radio to receive coded messages. The intent, CSIS believed, was to gather political, scientific, technological and military intelligence. The agency had some documented proof to go on: the real Ian MacKenzie Lambert had died at the age of three months, and the real Laurie Catherine Mary Brodie (the maiden name associated with "Laurie Lambert") had died just before her second birthday.

Yelena Olshevskaya and Dmitriy Olshevsky had entered Canada in the 1980s using forged documents. "Ian" arrived in Vancouver, moving to Montréal and then going to Toronto. He met "Laurie" and the two married, collected social insurance numbers, drivers licences and passports. The two had spent their time before coming to Canada learning their "legend," or the life under which they were to live in Canada, but that proved problematic in some cases. Ian sometimes forgot his middle name and his accent became more notable when he drank alcohol. On one occasion he was involved in a car crash where it was noted he was wearing his wedding ring on the wrong hand (Russians wear wedding rings on the right hand). Some of his colleagues wondered how a photo developer married to an insurance clerk could afford a Mazda MX-3 Precidia and live in such an upscale apartment building.

Two agents had tried to rent the apartment next door to the Lamberts but had failed. Farrell was the next person to try, and he succeeded. His job was to watch the Lamberts' comings and goings to determine the best time to perform a covert entry. He was able to listen through the walls to learn more about them— who got up first, who enjoyed longer showers and what time they typically left in the morning. The couple's mail was intercepted, but they received only bills;

no foreign correspondence. Six members of the Physical Surveillance Unit (PSU) were assigned to keep an eye on the pair.

In October 1994, courtesy of Farrell's work and the ongoing surveillance of the two spies, CSIS learned the couple was planning to travel out of town one weekend. In the days preceding, Farrell's apartment had been stuffed with the necessary surveillance gear. On Thursday night, after receiving the OK from the higher-ups, the SOS team moved in, planting bugs as well as video surveillance equipment in the Lamberts' home. When the team left, the apartment looked as if it had never been touched.

The resulting intelligence haul revealed that the sham marriage was disintegrating, in part because Ian was in love with another woman named Anita Keyes. Shortly after the entry was made, Ian moved to a shabby high-rise in Toronto's east end, and Laurie moved to a bachelor suite elsewhere. There was some suspicion that the marital separation had been manufactured by the SVR to throw CSIS off, but it later concluded the entire episode was genuine. Now CSIS had two separate people to watch.

CSIS teams rented a suite inside Laurie's new apartment building and set up an observation post in an apartment across the street from Ian's. Surveillance equipment was installed to monitor the two spies. The agency went further. One night, the agency simply stole Ian's car to plant bugs inside it. CSIS had planned to break into Ian's new apartment, but a janitor replacing light bulbs scared them off.

Before the team could try again, it received news that the Lamberts were being recalled to Russia briefly. Rather than waiting until they returned, CSIS in co-operation with the RCMP, decided to pounce before the couple left, just in case Russia wasn't planning on sending them back to Canada. On May 22, 1996, the RCMP arrested Ian while he was trying to move his car. That same day, Laurie was simply plucked off the street on her way to work. CSIS promptly cleaned out both apartments, looking for any materials or intelligence that could bolster its case. Five days later, the story broke, and CSIS was crowing, finally trotting out a successful operation to boost its poor image. The government was prepared to deport the pair but had little public evidence on which to act. In the end, both Russians saved them the hassle; they admitted to being spies and were summarily flown back to Moscow.

It was never revealed exactly what tipped CSIS off that the Lamberts might have been spies. One rumour is that a Russian defector provided it with some general information that led to the pair. The agency also learned that a municipal clerk in Québec had typed Laurie Brodie's name into the computer for some sort of search and was notified of the existence of both a death certificate and an active social insurance number on file.

At the time, CSIS was starting to focus on other issues that were emerging as well. One was "single-issue terrorism" and the groups associated with it that devoted the bulk of their resources to ventures related to the environment, the fur trade and other causes. These types of groups had been present for years, but an incident in early 1996 demonstrated that some organizations were willing to take their agendas to a more violent level. In January of that year, a group calling itself the "Justice Department" started sending letters in the mail to people involved in the fur trade. Each letter contained a razor blade that a note inside the envelope stated was covered in HIV-infected blood. Hundreds of people received the envelopes, from retail executives to hunters. Analysis of the razor blades quickly determined that the people who had received the letters were not at risk of contracting HIV, but the letter campaign illustrated to CSIS what the single-issue terrorists were capable of doing.

A report released after the incident stated that there was evidence for real concern about what such small groups associated predominately with environmental and animal rights issues could do. Their activities, CSIS concluded, would most likely take the shape of vandalism, acts of arson and the use of bombs. The number of people willing to use these means, CSIS believed, was ultimately small.

Similar reports detailed growing anger over bio-engineering and genetically modified crops—cereals, vegetables and fruits grown from seeds that were scientifically designed, for example, to produce more robust crops with built-in immunities to the diseases and pests that typically decimated their ranks. In 2001, one group against genetically modified organisms (GMOs) attacked several corn plots on an experimental farm in Ottawa, causing $50,000 worth of damage. However, the corn on those particular plots was not of the genetically modified variety. CSIS warned that a cycle of anger could lead to waves of protests, demonstrations and other acts of destruction against genetically modified crops and vegetation. Two years before the corn incident, 500 trees at a University of British Columbia research facility had been attacked. A group called Reclaim the Genes took responsibility for the assault.

There was also the enduring issue of Operation Sidewinder, a joint CSIS–RCMP investigation specifically designed in the mid-1990s to study the potential influence of Chinese business in Canada. It was believed that these same business people were donating money to political parties in order to influence certain politicians when it came to government foreign and domestic trade policy. The report examined the links these businessmen had to triads (Chinese organized crime gangs), which were establishing a foothold in Canada, and whether or not some individuals were actually members of the People's Liberation Army (PLA; Chinese military) and were, by extension, spies. There were reports that a batch of weapons confiscated from a Canadian Mohawk reserve had been manufactured by a Chinese company. In effect, Sidewinder was looking for evidence of persuasion, illegal activity and the possibility that Chinese-run businesses were being used as fronts for technical, economic and military espionage in Canada.

Although the two agencies worked together on the case, the RCMP was shocked and angered when CSIS issued its final report. The RCMP maintained that CSIS had watered down or entirely omitted some of the intelligence the Mounties had collected. The Mounties' protests amounted to little because, in 1997, Operation Sidewinder was ordered shut down. Revised versions of the interim report were distributed, but CSIS insisted that none of the information it had come across suggested anything more than conspiracy theories with no supporting evidence.

There was a small outcry as employees of both CSIS and the RCMP began to suspect political involvement by Prime Minister Jean Chrétien who, before assuming office, had worked for several Chinese companies with assets inside Canada. The allegations, however, were never substantially proven.

Sidewinder remained a sore spot for CSIS for years afterward, especially as successive reports to Parliament named a specific country as being aggressively involved in espionage inside Canada over an accumulating succession of years. Although its name had been, for national security reasons, redacted from public versions of the report, the evidence clearly pointed to China. Yet no information had come forward or been released that definitively proved that Chinese businesses were exerting unwarranted pressure on members of the Canadian government, that the Chinese government was using these same businesses to secure economic and trade secrets or that the country was employing spies to conduct espionage inside Canada's borders.

Many people disputed the decision to prematurely terminate the Sidewinder probe. The operation again came to light when newly minted RCMP Commissioner Giuliano Zaccardelli gave a speech to reporters and claimed criminal organizations were intent on disrupting Canada's Parliament. His claim triggered a SIRC report on Operation Sidewinder which, in the tradition of SIRC reports, stated that nothing untoward had occurred and that the operation had not been terminated as believed—it was merely "delayed because its initial product proved to be inadequate." Many Canadians disagreed.

Although all 30 copies of the interim report were ordered destroyed, along with the background notes, a few copies ended up in the hands of the opposition and the press. The report asserted that businessmen, triads and Chinese intelligence agencies had been working with their government for 15 years and that some of their activities in Canada were intended to cover up criminal or intelligence activities. In the report, such pursuits as money laundering, heroin trafficking and the transfer of intelligence of all stripes were linked to mainland China. The report maintained that China has "obtained access" to influential persons previously or currently active in high levels of Canadian society. No further action was taken, courtesy of SIRC, which absolved CSIS of any responsibility or wrongdoing.

CSIS Structure

As the 21st century dawned, CSIS' core structure was essentially intact, as were its hiring procedures, even though budget cuts under the federal Liberal government of Jean Chrétien had trimmed approximately 800 people from the agency. The top and most public face of CSIS is its director, who oversees all aspects of the agency's day-to-day operations. As of 2005, the director reports the activities of the intelligence service to the Minister of Public Safety Canada.

At CSIS' core is the Counter-Intelligence Branch, which monitors threats from other intelligence agencies around the world. That branch is divided into Security and Information, Security Information Operations and Transnational Crime and Foreign Influence sections. There are three programs within Security and Information—one provides security clearances for government employees, one screens foreigners at the request of other governments and another screens the backgrounds of would-be immigrants and refugees for Citizenship and Immigration Canada. Security clearances, especially for government positions, differ on the secrecy level of the information a worker needs to see, and there are three clearance levels: confidential, secret and top-secret. In the early 2000s, Front End Screening was implemented to check out the backgrounds of refugees as quickly as possible.

CSIS also includes numerous other branches, all dedicated to the similar goal of protecting Canada, but with responsibilities for different parts of it.

Sharing intelligence with other agencies is particularly important given that Canada does not have a foreign intelligence agency. In total, CSIS has 250 co-operative agreements in place with organizations based in more than 200 countries.

Of particular interest and usefulness at CSIS is the preparation and production of National Intelligence Threat Assessments, reports that take into account emerging threats on a global and local scale over time periods of up to 15 years. The Integrated Threat Assessment Centre (ITAC) is responsible for providing comprehensive threat assessments that can be shared with and distributed to other Canadian agencies, such as other members of the intelligence community and first-responders such as the police. Responses to specific threats are evaluated in order to prevent or at least minimize the risk of a potential threat to Canadian security.

ITAC is a central-processing centre for intelligence obtained by almost a dozen other agencies, and the information is subsequently shared. Representatives of ITAC include not just CSIS but Public Safety Canada, the Canada Border Service Agency, the Communications Security Establishment, Department of National Defence, Foreign Affairs and International Trade Canada, the Privy Council Office, Transport Canada, Correctional Service Canada, Financial Transactions and Reports Analysis Centre of Canada, the RCMP, the Ontario Provincial Police and the Sûreté du Québec. For help in preparing its threat assessments, ITAC engages in partnerships with similar agencies based in other countries, including Great Britain, the United States, Australia and New Zealand.

The entire intelligence process, according to CSIS, is a five-step cycle that starts with the government of the day and ends with the dissemination of the end-product. The Minister of Public Safety Canada directs CSIS' activities according to the government's current and future priorities. CSIS then engages in a thorough planning cycle, starting with the construction of a threat assessment and culminating in a more detailed plan of action on how to actually deliver the end-product. CSIS then collects information via a variety of channels: open-source publications such as newspapers, periodicals and foreign and domestic broadcasts; Canadian partners in intelligence; interviews; the use of human sources; direct investigative techniques; and the interception of communications. Where necessary, CSIS can use Security Liaison Officers (SLOs) who are posted at diplomatic missions abroad to contact foreign intelligence agencies that might have information on any particular threat to Canada.

Once the information and intelligence have been gathered from all possible sources, the analysts use the information and their own expertise or the expertise of others within the agency to discern on a confidence level what the intelligence actually means and what action the government should take as a result. Sometimes this action includes conducting more threat assessments and intelligence reports. Depending on the department involved, CSIS states it can tailor the information it collects to provide a robust analysis of the issues specifically affecting any particular department. The information is then shared with any agency or government through the process of dissemination. Government departments, other intelligence and policing units and foreign intelligence agencies are most often on the receiving end of the cycle. This allows them to develop a more coherent policy in order to deal with the threats of the day. It also promotes a co-operative approach to maintaining the security of Canada through sharing with other police agencies such as the RCMP or with friendly intelligence agencies, again by using SLOs posted overseas.

The Hiring Process

Many positions are available to CSIS agents, but most require extensive education and world experience. Analysts must have a minimum of a master's degree, five years of experience in a particular field and a long list of scholarly publications in order to demonstrate a level of expertise in any specific discipline.

The backbone of the security service, however, is its intelligence officers (IO), and the application process can take upwards of a year to authorize someone for employment with CSIS. Each applicant must complete several steps before he or she can be officially hired. IOs are the grunts of the agency—they carry out overt and covert operations, interview community members to allow them to voice their concerns, develop threat assessments, conduct security screening, prepare warrants and engage in some espionage activity. IOs look for information that, after being processed by others at CSIS, becomes intelligence if it is deemed useful.

Inside the intelligence service, mentoring is relied upon heavily as a way to bring a junior employee up to speed. Only so much can be learned in the classroom—younger IOs are always paired with more senior co-workers to help refine their skills and learn the minuscule but important tricks of the trade.

When it comes to IOs, CSIS, like any other organization or business, recruits the best available. Anyone can fill out the application form online, and doing so triggers a series of steps that can either stop immediately based on the information in the application or move a candidate along farther to a sequential series of new steps.

At the beginning of the application stage, everyone who fills out the online form must meet three criteria—be a Canadian citizen, have a post-secondary degree and possess a driver's licence. According to former Prairie region Chief of Human Resources Emil Spilchak in a 2003 interview, the last criterion can often be the most problematic.

"You'd be surprised at the number of times I've had to say, 'Go get a licence, then we'll talk.'"

Officers such as Spilchak review all the completed applications, which are subsequently evaluated for the applicant's skills and work experience and are matched against the agency's needs. IOs are not the only employees at the agency—scientists, engineers, librarians and translators are also required. Individuals who speak multiple languages (besides English and French) are especially coveted. Furthermore, evidence of life experience has to be shown—the average hiring age is pegged at 27 years.

"The reality is we're looking for something more. If you just graduated university and live with mom and dad, we'll probably tell you to come back later," Spilchak said.

Applicants who pass this first stage must then fill out a more detailed application form and, once it is submitted, the agency contacts the applicant for the first of four interviews. The first is a forum through which the agency can assess the attributes of the individual.

"There are certain skills we are looking for in people, skills we know from experience are necessary. It's not rocket science; we're looking for you to impress us," Spilchak adds.

A passing grade in the first interview triggers an interview with a CSIS-employed psychologist who looks for more than just signs of depression or anxiety.

"We're looking at this interview from the perspective of determining the person's motivation. We want to know if they're hiding something or if their motivation isn't genuine," said Spilchak.

An "OK" from the CSIS shrinks leads to two more interviews—one with two senior staff members of the agency and another with a member of CSIS' executive branch. A passing grade on both means that the applicant moves on to the next step of the hiring process, which involves a massive background search of the individual's life, going back as far as 10 years. Agents seek out former employers, friends, teachers, neighbours and family members to determine if anything in the applicant's past could be used against them in the form of blackmail.

"It could be a financial thing. An investigator could come back and say, 'This guy has so much debt, he has no hope of ever paying it off, even on our salary,'" said Spilchak.

Another part of the security investigation is the controversial use of a polygraph machine for a "lie-detector test." The machine does not actually detect lies but measures physiological changes so that they can be compared with those typically associated with individuals telling mistruths. SIRC has stated it believes CSIS relies on the machine too much, both in its hiring process and in the course of its investigations, and polygraph results have created problems for the agency. Still, Spilchak said the agency believes when it comes to hiring, CSIS can't be too careful.

"It's a very intrusive investigation. Some of this stuff people might get embarrassed about, but we need to know everything."

If the background check comes back clean and no deviations are observed on the polygraph results, a candidate is finally approved to be offered a job with CSIS. In total, from initial application to approval, the average applicant can expect to wait 8–10 months before being offered a position. New recruits who require upgrading in either of Canada's two official languages are enrolled in language training. Following the satisfactory completion of this requirement, IOs receive 12 weeks of training in a classroom setting before beginning their mandatory two-year stint at CSIS headquarters in Ottawa. New hires are tasked predominately with preparing warrants authorizing invasive investigative techniques, such as electronic surveillance and mail opening.

"The threat has to be of such a magnitude as to justify intrusive means," Spilchak said. "To do that we need to be able to convince a federal judge to sign off on it."

Once they have completed their two years in Ottawa, IOs can be transferred to regional offices where they are trained as investigators. Their duties can include monitoring the media and using inform- ants and agents in order to accumulate as much raw information as possible about potential security threats to Canada and its allies. Agents may also serve overseas as part of CSIS' foreign liaison program to help foreign governments identify and counter threats within their borders that could also potentially exist in Canada.

CHAPTER NINE

Intelligence Shift

THE APPROACH OF THE NEW MILLENNIUM had everyone—from higher-ups to regular residents—scrambling. Doomsday cults predicted the end of the world. The ominous threat of Y2K hung over what was supposed to be the celebration of a lifetime. At its worst, Y2K adherents packed up survival supplies, expecting the total collapse of the world's computer communication systems that would lead to inadvertent nuclear missile launches, massive power outages, airplanes falling out of the sky and so on. None of it came to pass, and the world entered the 21st century ready to embrace a promising future.

Along Canada's western border, however, a man with a drastically different plan for the future would soon be arrested and charged with a scheme so potentially deadly it would have thrust the world into a new era of fear.

In the history of North America, no foreign entity had managed to conduct a terrorist attack on American or Canadian soil. The FLQ bombings of the October Crisis were committed by entirely home-grown individuals. The Oklahoma City bombing of

1995, although devastating, was carried out by a gun-toting, freedom-loving American citizen. Terror was reserved for points overseas, for the Middle East as Arab nations joined with the Palestinian people in their ongoing war against Israel and its allies. Bombs were commonplace in the Middle East, as were random shootings.

U.S. and Canadian troops, however, had been targets of terrorist attacks while serving overseas in foreign, potentially hostile countries—the most tragic example being the 1983 bombing of the U.S. Marine barracks in Lebanon that killed 241 American servicemen, an attack that Libya eventually admitted to 15 years after the fact. The same attack killed 58 French servicemen in a separate building. But such an attack had never occurred on home soil. One man living in Canada was setting out to change that.

Montréal is one of Canada's cultural hotspots. Although predominately French, which is no surprise given that it is the largest population centre in Québec, Montréal also contains small communities of refugees and landed immigrants from dozens of countries within its boundaries. Restaurant fare is not the only indicator of Montréal's multicultural face—various parts of town are named for the congregation of specific nationalities. Although it is not uncommon for many North American cities to have a Chinatown or Little Italy, Montréal has a long list of ethnic neighbourhoods comprising its rich tapestry of culture.

One man living in Montréal prior to the turn of the 21st century was Ahmed Ressam, a 33-year-old resident who originally came to Canada in 1994 from his native Algeria. Ressam, however, was no ordinary refugee. He was an active Islamic militant, sent to Canada with the specific purpose of mounting a terrorist attack on North American soil. He originally claimed political asylum when he came to Canada, stating he would most likely be tortured or killed if he was returned to Algeria.

He became a petty thief in Montréal, stealing whatever he could get his hands on. He was arrested in Montréal for pick-pocketing senior citizens at a local Sears but was released without charge. He was picked up for stealing luggage at Vancouver International Airport but again—because of his phony passport—he wasn't taken into custody. When he didn't show up for his refugee hearing, his application for refugee status was subsequently denied. However, Ressam was able to obtain another fraudulent passport under the name Benni Noris, with the result that the authorities were unable to locate him again. All the while, he was living in Canada with another known terrorist, a man named Karim Said Atmani, a document forger belonging to the Algeria-based Groupe Islamique Armé.

In 1998, barely four years after sneaking his way into Canada, Ressam was able to sneak out. His destination was one that had become increasingly popular with militant factions across the world that were determined to wreak havoc within North America— Afghanistan. The Islamic government of the Taliban had emerged from the ruins of the Soviet occupation and taken control of the nation, enforcing its own strict interpretation of Islam and *sharia* (Islamic law based on the Koran). The Taliban were also friendly to terrorist organizations of the Islamic faith, particularly that of al-Qaeda, which was financed and directed by former Saudi prince Osama bin Laden.

Bin Laden was well known in intelligence circles and had come to the forefront of the public eye when militants detonated truck bombs outside embassies in Kenya and Tanzania in 1998. The U.S. government had responded to the attacks with a series of cruise missile strikes on suspected bases of operation, but bin Laden was still alive and freely operating at the pleasure of the Taliban and its one-eyed leader, Mullah Mohammed Omar. Financed by bin Laden himself and Taliban-friendly organizations the world over, camps dedicated to training terrorists had sprung up throughout Afghanistan.

Not all of the camps were geared toward al-Qaeda recruits specifically—they trained future terrorists for numerous other Islamic militant movements. Ressam was one of these men, leaving Canada in 1998 to train at the Khalden training camp with another roommate, Mustapha Labsi. During the pair's time in Afghanistan, they learned all about using weapons, manufacturing explosives and the other basics of terror.

CSIS was aware of Ressam's presence in Canada, but his trip to Afghanistan went completely unnoticed by the organization. Because the Algerian was travelling under a false name and passport, the agency had no way of knowing where he was at any given time. All it knew as 1998 wore into 1999 was that Ressam was nowhere to be found.

When Ressam returned to Canada in 1999, he immediately set himself up in a Burnaby, BC, motel. There, he and an associate started working on a bomb. He worked diligently and persistently, repeatedly refusing maid service as he prepared his device for its intended target—Los Angeles International Airport (LAX). On December 14, 1999, a little more than two weeks before the millennium, Ressam left his room and drove to Victoria, where he boarded the MV *Coho*, the ferry operated by Black Ball Line, to transit the Strait of Juan de Fuca to Port Angeles, Washington. U.S. customs agents in Victoria had questioned Ressam but cleared him to board the ferry; he had to again clear U.S. customs once he arrived in Port Angeles. At the time, U.S. border control agent Diana Dean, stationed at Port Angeles, observed, "I don't recall any specific threats. I don't recall anybody saying watch for terrorists."

U.S. customs officials later confirmed that no alert had been sent to the field.

Still, when Ressam pulled up to speak with U.S. customs officials, he appeared nervous. When asked to provide identification, he handed them a Costco membership card. His rented vehicle was taken aside for a thorough inspection by customs officials. As they searched his clothing, Ressam escaped, but he was soon recaptured.

What the inspectors found inside the vehicle shocked the world—the spare tire well was packed with explosives and four timing devices. The luggage Ressam was carrying tested positive for trace quantities of explosive materials. A search of the car turned up a Canadian passport with a fake name and the phone number for a man named Abdel Ghani, an American living in the New York area who had helped Ressam compile some of the necessary ingredients for his bomb and who was waiting for him in the United States at a Best Western hotel. The Joint Terrorism Task Force arrested Ghani two weeks later in Brooklyn and took him into custody.

News of Ressam's arrest caught North America by surprise. The media instantly dubbed him the "Millennium Bomber," and U.S. officials pointed the finger at Canada for its porous borders and lax immigration procedures.

It was revealed that CSIS had actually begun watching Ressam in 1996 as part of a larger probe into Islamic extremists in Canada. CSIS had discovered that Ressam was associated with a Bosnian War veteran in Montréal who believed he was engaged in a holy war against the United States.

At the time, CSIS had filed a warrant with a federal court judge to tap the phone in Ressam's home, and it was granted. The conversations revealed that Ressam and his tiny cell were aiding other terrorist cells in countries such as Turkey, Italy and France. The agency learned of his plans to attend training camps in Afghanistan but were unable to do anything about it except alert the U.S. authorities and the RCMP.

But neither CSIS nor the Mounties knew where to look. Through a little bit of ingenuity and persuasiveness, Ressam had managed to apply for and receive a passport under a fake name. First, he had obtained a baptismal certificate and forged the signature of a known Catholic priest, then he doctored up a Université de Montréal student identification card and presented both items as supporting evidence for a passport. It was because of this passport that CSIS had no idea where Ressam actually was once he left the country for Afghanistan. They only learned that he had returned when he was arrested at Port Angeles.

In total, Ressam was charged with nine counts in the United States, including engaging in international terrorism, smuggling explosives, using false documents and possession of stolen documents. He was brought to trial in 2001, and CSIS was asked to help in the prosecution by providing whatever evidence it had on Ressam's time in Canada. Unfortunately, CSIS' penchant for stepping on its own toes landed it in hot water with the presiding judge. The courts disallowed a report complied by CSIS when it was revealed that CSIS had destroyed the original audio recordings concerning Ressam's trip to Afghanistan to take part in terrorist training. To try to salvage that portion of their case, the U.S. attorneys prosecuting Ressam asked the judge to let the translator who had worked on the tapes to testify via video link, on the condition the translator be allowed to share information with the court anonymously.

The judge, however, ruled against the idea of letting someone testify before the court without allowing the defendant to face his accuser. Although the judge had some stinging rebukes for the quality of professionalism displayed by CSIS, in the end, the report didn't matter: in 2001, a jury found Ressam guilty on all counts.

His sentencing, however, was postponed for almost four years. In 2001 he began co-operating with investigators, giving information that revealed that al-Qaeda had set up several "sleeper cells" within North America, especially in the United States. These sleepers were instructed to lie low within the country and attempt to blend in as much as possible until they received instructions on what role they would play in an attack. Many of Ressam's statements were used in a President's Daily Brief presented to United States President George W. Bush on August 6, 2001; it was entitled *Bin Laden Determined to Strike in U.S.* Of 36 briefs presented to Bush over the preceding year, it was the first to warn that the al-Qaeda leader was trying to organize a terrorist attack within the United States.

The brief also mentioned the target cities of New York and Washington and stated that hijacking an aircraft to demand the release of prisoners would be involved. This document would later be used to criticize the United States intelligence community for failing to take more aggressive steps to prevent the tragedies of September 11, 2001.

Ressam gave evidence in front of a group known as the Guantanamo Bay Combatant Status Review

Tribunal that decided whether or not certain individuals should be designated "unlawful enemy combatants" after having been captured in combat in Afghanistan and shipped to the notorious holding facility. One individual who testified at the tribunal stated that when Ressam went to Afghanistan, the camp he attended was used only for fighters committed to the idea of "defensive jihad," striking only military targets. He stated that attacks geared toward killing and injuring civilians were an offence to Islam itself, and, given the nature of the Khalden camp, Ressam never would have been accepted if anyone at the camp had thought he was actually planning an attack against the civilian population. Furthermore, although Ressam had become fairly "radicalized" while living in Montréal, he became more fanatical after he left the camp, the informant suggested.

After co-operating with authorities for several years, Ressam suddenly experienced a change of heart. The *Seattle Times* reported that "Ressam underwent a second transformation to emerge as a silent, uncooperative prisoner who said he only wanted to be left alone and finally learn his fate."

His sentence was finally handed down in 2005. After apologizing to the judge for his role in the millennium bomb plot, Ressam learned that he would spend the next 22 years behind bars, even though the U.S. government was petitioning the court for a sentence as long as 35 years. Ressam's lawyers later appealed, winning a split decision in the United States Court of Appeals for the Ninth Circuit that reversed a conviction on the charges and sent the case back for resentencing. The lawyers lost a subsequent appeal to the Supreme Court of the United States that over-turned the appeals court's decision in 2008 and restored the original conviction.

On February 2, 2010, the same appeals court set Ressam's sentence aside, stating in a split decision that the original sentencing judge had been too lenient when he slapped the millennium bomber with 22 years in jail. They took the case one step farther and stated Ressam should be resentenced by a different judge because the one who oversaw his original trial failed to weigh the need to protect the public in deciding Ressam's sentence.

"The factor is particularly relevant in a terrorist case such as this, where Ressam, who has demonstrated strongly held beliefs about the need to attack American interests in the United States and abroad, will be only 53 years old upon his release," the majority of the court ruled.

Ressam has since recanted "every word" he ever spoke while giving information to intelligence agencies from the United States, Canada, Britain, Italy, France, Spain and Germany. "I did not know what I was saying," Ressam said, adding that the FBI was putting words in his mouth.

Ressam's case was further proof that Canada's position in the world was changing. Immigrants weren't just raising funds for out-of-country organizations and offering support but were using Canada as a base where terrorists could plan and organize attacks on North American targets. Those sentiments were supported in a report issued in March 2000 that, citing the Ressam case as an example, proved terrorists were starting to view Canada differently. It had long been a base where terrorist groups often solicited funds from local émigré populations and transferred the money to support the violent causes in their home countries overseas.

The Liberation Tigers of Tamil Eelam (LTTE), the terrorist group in Sri Lanka engaged in a bloody civil war for independence since 1983, had several fundraising factions in Canada operating under the guise of being non-profit support groups. The Tigers proved to be one of Canada's top fundraisers. Yet, despite evidence that the funds were being sent to fuel the war in Sri Lanka, the Canadian government was not willing to crackdown on the Tigers, nor on other groups suspected of raising funds and support for other terrorist organizations such as Hamas (Palestine) or Hezbollah (Lebanon).

The Tigers' presence in Canada was particularly embarrassing. In January 1996, the LTTE detonated a bomb at the Central Bank in Colombo, Sri Lanka, killing 86 people and injuring 1400 others. It turned out that the explosives used in the attack were purchased with money from an account traced back to a Canadian. CSIS had recognized for several years that the Tigers were using both legal and illegal methods in Canada to raise funds, but the government of the day—the Liberal Party of Canada—refused to take action. Moreover, some members of the Liberal Party seemed to support the Tiger cause.

Several Members of Parliament were spotted at LTTE fundraisers and then–Finance Minister Paul Martin had spoken at a fundraising dinner for the Federal Association of Canadian Tamils, believed to be a front organization for the LTTE. Other organizations seemed especially well connected, including the World Tamil Movement, which was also believed to be raising money in Canada for the war. The World Tamil Movement received an $18,000 government grant to hire a volunteer co-ordinator, even though CSIS had deemed the co-ordinator of the group, Manickavasagam Suresh, to be a security threat in 1995, after he had been in the country for five years. Suresh was subsequently arrested and deported, but no action was taken against any of the Tamil groups. "LTTE activities undermine Canada's responsibility to ensure the safety and security of the Canadian people," noted Rand Corporation consultant Peter Chalk.

Some members of Canada's Tamil community started to engage in blatant criminal activity that led to bloody, often lethal confrontations between devout supporters and moderates in Canadian cities. One gang established itself under the name VVT and used the proceeds it generated from drug trafficking and fraud to help fund the LTTE cause in Sri Lanka. The gang dealt harshly with dissenting Tamils in Canada who chose not to donate to the cause. Over the course of three years in the late 1990s, 40 Tamil gang shootings and five unsolved homicides were linked to the ethnic group. In 1999, collectively the fundraising groups of the LTTE managed to raise approximately $12 million and procure another $10 million in business revenues, all of which was believed to have been shipped to Sri Lanka to support the Tigers.

Canada made a big show of signing the 1999 UN Convention for the Suppression of Financing of Terrorism, but by 2001 we had still not passed any domestic laws to honour the agreement. Within the global community, Canada was seen as a place where terrorist groups could raise money with relative ease. The Ressam case had demonstrated that other groups could use the country as a base for logistical planning and organization. Despite CSIS' reports highlighting these facts, no substantive policy changes ever came to light under the rule of the Liberals.

And then on September 11, 2001, the entire world watched as a devoted group of terrorists seized control of four airplanes in the United States and used them as fuel-filled missiles that killed thousands of innocent civilians. Osama bin Laden claimed responsibility for the attack. The entire intelligence community of the United States—and the rest of the Western world—was caught completely by surprise, and no one could predict what might come next. For the first time in history, foreign terrorists had struck the North American homeland in a very cruel and spectacular way. The focus of espionage had suddenly shifted, and Canada especially had to take action if it wanted to provide its agencies and departments with the tools they needed to fight terrorism at home and abroad.

Several Canadians died in the 9/11 attacks, but it wasn't the human element that finally spurred the government to action. Infuriated members of the U.S. Congress unequivocally claimed that the terrorists had to have come from Canada, given our lax immigration standards. Canada's police and security establishments quickly investigated and proved that none of the hijackers had spent any time in the country or had received any assistance from anyone within its borders. Still, it was a possibility that Canada, much like in the Ressam case, could be a jumping-off point in the future. That Osama bin Laden named Canada as a target nation in one of his audio recordings released to the public also meant that CSIS needed more tools—technology, agents and legislative mechanisms—if it was going to keep Canadians safe. What followed was one of the most controversial pieces of legislation ever passed by Parliament.

It started as Bill C-36 and later became known as the Anti-terrorism Act. The omnibus bill proposed myriad amendments to legislation that already existed, including the Criminal Code and the Immigration Act, in order to better protect Canadians against terrorism. The bill was introduced shortly after the 9/11 attacks and received royal assent in December of that same year. Although the government maintained that the bill struck the right balance between protecting Canadians and guarding their individual rights and freedoms, it soon became the topic of controversy as civil libertarians denounced it as an infringement of the Charter of Rights and

Freedoms, and several of its core components were appealed all the way to the Supreme Court of Canada.

As passed, the Anti-terrorism Act gave teeth to two conventions to which Canada was signatory—but had failed to act on domestically. The first was the Convention for the Suppression of Financing of Terrorism, a United Nations' agreement that calls for freezing properties and funds believed to be used to finance terrorist activity and making it illegal to fund terrorists. The government backed up its commitment to the convention by amending the Criminal Code to create laws that prohibited financing terrorism and gave Federal Court judges the power to order the freezing, seizure and forfeiture of property used in or related to terrorist activities.

The second convention, the Convention for the Suppression of Terrorist Bombings, contains provisions that deal with terrorist groups targeting public places, government or infrastructure with explosives or other lethal devices.

The Criminal Code also included a host of new offences specifically designed to combat terrorism. Terrorist activity was defined in the code as an "action taken for political, religious or ideological reasons to intimidate the public and government of the day into doing or not doing something by intentionally causing the deaths, harming or endangering the lives of people, damaging property in a way that is likely to harm other people or by disrupting an essential service, facility or system."

The Anti-terrorism Act was quick to spell out that simply exercising one's right to free expression on political, religious or ideological grounds was not a terrorist activity unless it was accompanied by a violent action as defined above. The act created a list of groups whose activities met the definition of a terrorist group. Several new offences under the Criminal Code were included:

- knowingly participating or contributing to an activity of a terrorist group

- knowingly facilitating a terrorist activity

- knowingly instructing anyone to carry out a terrorist activity (alone or in connection with a group)

- knowingly harbouring or concealing a terrorist

All of these offences were named as "primary designated offences," meaning that anyone convicted of a crime under any of the terrorism-related charges had to provide a DNA sample to the authorities.

The Anti-terrorism Act included several amendments designed to make it easier for CSIS, the RCMP and other police forces to collect evidence and prevent terrorist activity. While electronic surveillance of any kind still required the approval of a Federal Court judge, engaging in such activity no longer had to be considered as the last resort. Whereas wiretap warrants had earlier been valid for only 60 days, the act extended that time frame to one year when police are investigating a possible terrorist group offence.

As well, the requirement that police had to notify subjects of electronic surveillance that they had been the target of such investigation could be delayed for up to three years. Police officers could now apply to a court for an investigative hearing requiring an individual with information relevant to an ongoing terrorist investigation to provide it to the court. The government balanced this requirement with the condition that approval of the Attorney General had to be obtained before the hearing could take place.

But the most significant policing power the act addressed was when police could make an arrest. The legislation introduced the power of "preventative arrest" for police officers across the country. A peace officer could now arrest and detain an individual for a short period of time if the officer believed on reasonable grounds that a terrorist activity would be carried out and the officer suspected that arresting the person was necessary to prevent terrorist activity. Before the act was introduced, police could arrest individuals only after they had committed a crime. A police officer with reasonable suspicion that a terrorist attack was imminent could now legally take an individual into custody in order to prevent an attack and could hold the suspect behind bars for an indefinite period of time.

New laws extended within the government and security service as well. Under the Security of Information Act (formerly the Official Secrets Act), any person who communicated classified information to another person without authorization could be jailed for up to 14 years. This act applied especially to individuals such as CSIS agents who are permanently bound to secrecy, whether still employed by the agency or not, as a part of their oath upon employment. Amendments to the Canada Evidence Act made it easer for the Attorney General to declare certain information used in court proceedings too sensitive to share with the public because it could be a threat to national defence or national security.

The Communications Security Establishment (CSE) received new responsibilities too, including using and acquiring intelligence from the intercepted communications of foreign targets (part of its mandate to begin with), as well as giving advice, guidance and services to the government to help protect Canada's "electronic infrastructure" or sensitive computer systems from vandalism, interference or theft. The CSE, which had been prohibited from spying on Canadians within the country's borders, could now do so to assist the RCMP or CSIS with an ongoing investigation.

Significantly, the Proceeds of Crime (Money Laundering) and Terrorist Financing Act was amended to allow the Financial Transactions and Reports and Analysis Centre (FINTRAC) to look for financial transactions that might be related to terrorist activities and to share the information with the appropriate authorities. The Charities Registration (Security Information) Act was created to help the government deal with terrorist-sponsored organizations established within Canada as charities. The new act allowed the government to deny support to any entity listed as a charity that was found to be using its status to fund terrorist organizations or activities.

The Liberal government also beefed up the Criminal Code with new amendments targeting hate crimes and hate propaganda. Judges are now able to order the deletion of hate propaganda from Internet sites. The code also created a new offence of mischief that deemed any action motivated by bias or prejudice based on religion, race, colour or national or ethnic groups committed against places of worship or associated property, such as cemeteries, as a hate crime. The offence carries a maximum penalty of 10 years in prison on indictment or 18 months on summary conviction.

But the most controversial aspect of the Anti-terrorism Act actually has its roots in the Ministry of Immigration, courtesy of the Immigration and Refugee Protection Act. Under the system in place since the late 1970s, the government has the authority to issue a certificate against permanent residents or foreign nationals if they are deemed to be a threat to national security. A certificate, co-signed by the Solicitor General and the Minister of Citizenship and Immigration, allows for the immediate detention of the individual named within. The person is promptly taken before a judge in a secret court where neither the person nor his or her lawyers are able to review the evidence the government has brought before the court. If the judge rules the certificate is valid, the individual can be deported to his or her country of origin. If a judge rules the certificate is inadequate, the individual is released. The certificate was created in the first place to deal with immigrants who are inadmissible to Canada on grounds of "security, violating human or international rights, serious criminality or organized criminality."

Security certificates have been used in the past—to date, 29 have been issued, and most dealt with individuals with less-than-savoury backgrounds. Holocaust denier Ernst Zundel was the subject of a security certificate and was subsequently deported, as were foreign spies who did not leave the country willingly.

The Anti-terrorism Act seized on the security certificate system, and the government decided to include any foreign nationals suspected of involvement in a terrorist organization or terrorist activities as the subjects of such certificates. The entire idea of using certificates, however, was fraught with legal pitfalls. All individuals in Canada have the right, after being charged, to see the evidence against them in a public court. Security certificates don't necessarily involve charging a person with an offence; they only assert that the individual might pose a threat to Canadian national security. The person named on the certificate and that individual's lawyer are not allowed to see any of the evidence against them, on national security grounds. Furthermore, the proceedings are held in secret, contrary to Canada's belief in a public, open court system.

Critics feared that using the certificates gave the government the opportunity to abuse the process without any sort of oversight or judicial discretion. For all intents and purposes, so long as the judge was willing, the government could detain an individual for any length of time until the case was decided. Only permanent residents and foreign nationals—not Canadian citizens—can be detained under a security certificate.

The system of issuing security certificates was a controversial legal matter that inevitably wound up before the Supreme Court of Canada. On February 23, 2007, the court ruled unanimously that the use of security certificates was grossly unconstitutional. However, instead of simply quashing the entire process, the court suspended its judgement for a period of one year in order to allow the government to draw up a new law that included a better review process that would protect the rights of detainees. In early 2008, Parliament responded with a revised bill that allowed the security certificate system to continue. The new law created "special advocates," (lawyers) who had been security cleared and could attend a court hearing with their client, challenge government evidence and generally act to ensure that the rights of their client were being upheld during the proceedings.

The government introduced several other changes to the act to make it more palatable. These included the use of "sunset clauses" or powers that would automatically lapse three years after the bill was given royal assent if they were not renewed by Parliament. The clause specifically applied to amendments governing preventative arrest of suspected terrorists and investigative hearings. By a vote of Parliament, preventative arrests and investigative hearings were allowed to lapse in March 2007. Another amendment required the Attorney General and Minister of Public Safety to table annual reports to Parliament detailing the use of both powers.

In addition, the definition of "terrorist activity" was amended so that lawful protest activity was not lumped in with the definition. As well, the offence of facilitating a terrorist attack was changed to ensure that a person, in order to be found guilty of the offence, had to know that his or her actions would help a terrorist activity to occur. The Attorney General was able to sign a certificate designating information as sensitive to issues of national security only when a judge confirmed this assessment and not whenever the Attorney General felt like it.

The use of security certificates against foreign nationals, however, became the most controversial aspect of the entire process in the new fight against terrorism. And CSIS was looking for some way to help corral the flood of immigrants from countries that sponsored terrorism—the belief was that al-Qaeda and other terrorist organizations were quietly setting up sleeper cells inside Canada, sending refugees abroad to blend in before calling them to action. Some of the statistics behind immigration were alarming. For three years following the September 11 attacks in the United States, some 15,000 refugees came to Canada. Of that total, 2500 came from countries that were known to sponsor terrorism. More chilling still, of 200,000 refugees who entered the country illegally, 36,000 of them, many of whom had criminal backgrounds or could be considered a security risk, could not be located inside Canada.

CSIS released a report in December 2001 stating that no known al-Qaeda cells were in Canada, but that there was a small crop of supporters and sympathizers, numbering fewer than 100. Still, the subsequent war in Afghanistan sent those Canadians of the Islamic faith who believed in bin Laden's cause flying overseas for training at terrorist camps, but the government didn't know for certain how many, unless individuals were apprehended or somehow otherwise identified. Another grim statistic emerged by 2002, however, that stated al-Qaeda had dispersed some 10,000 trained operatives throughout the world, including some believed to have landed in Canada, who were sleeper agents, ready to strike when called upon to do so.

CSIS already had several targets on its radar— landed immigrants or permanent residents whom the agency had determined were somehow linked to a terrorist organization and wanted to see deported from the country, or at least removed from the streets. Using the security certificate provisions granted under the Immigration and Refugee Protection Act, CSIS quickly descended on a group of individuals who later became known as "The Secret Trial Five."

Hassan Almrei, born in Syria on January 1, 1974, had arrived in Canada in 1999, claiming refugee status. CSIS plucked him off the streets in October 2001 after a security certificate was issued for his detention and deportation.

Almrei was raised in Saudi Arabia. When he was seven, one of his uncles was sent to jail for 10 years for his role in the Muslim Brotherhood terrorist organization. Almrei's father had been tried in absentia and convicted of membership in the Muslim Brotherhood in the family's homeland of Syria and sentenced to death. Growing up with eight siblings, Almrei had been a devout Muslim since an early age, apparently memorizing the Koran while he was still very young. After high school, he spent several months doing office work for a charitable organization called the Muslim Africa Agency, then decided to become one of the *mujahideen*, or freedom-fighters, in Afghanistan, fighting off the "Communist-backed troops and rival forces." He first attended a camp run by Abdul Rasul Sayyaf, a commander in the Northern Alliance that opposed the rule of the Taliban and was fighting for control of the country. In total, Almrei made three trips to Afghanistan before travelling to Pakistan in 1994 and Yemen in 1995.

In 1998, after dabbling in the honey business, which CSIS has maintained has been a popular front for funnelling money to terrorist organizations overseas, Almrei applied to immigrate to Canada but was rebuked. Instead he went to Thailand and met a human trafficker named Ghaled who furnished Almrei with a forged United Arab Emirates passport that he quickly destroyed after arriving in Canada in January 1999.

Almrei was subsequently spotted with a group of five other men in September of that same year in a restricted area at Pearson Airport in Toronto. According to information filed with his security certificate later on, the group seemed to have codes and access cards for the area, but Almrei argued that he and the other men were working a temporary job at the airport and had permission to be in the area. In 2000, Almrei went on to buy a small restaurant franchise, but within the year he sold it for less than he had paid for it.

Meanwhile, CSIS was becoming suspicious of Almrei. There had been numerous instances where associates of Almrei were found in possession of forged travel documents. CSIS interviewed him and took the liberty of searching his computer. They found photos of Muslim guerrilla fighter Emir Khattab, Osama bin Laden and September 11 hijacker Mohammed Atta on his computer. Almrei was interviewed again by CSIS in the presence of his lawyer and denied that the photos were anything more than cached copies of BBC articles he had recently read. He denied allegations that he had travelled to Sudan, Afghanistan, Tajikistan, Uzbekistan, Azerbaijan, Dagestan or Chechnya.

Nonetheless, CSIS agents produced a security certificate in October 2001 and took him into custody. The following month, a federal court judge ruled in a secret hearing that the certificate was reasonable. Almrei tried to amend his statement, saying that he had been in Afghanistan as an imam (the Islam equivalent of a priest or church leader) and in Tajikistan to run a girls' school, but the government placed him in custody at the Toronto West Detention Centre.

While there, Almrei staged two hunger strikes, one lasting 39 days so that he could obtain winter clothing and shoes, and a 73-day hunger strike in an effort to obtain one hour of exercise per day. After intervening in a prisoner assault on a guard, Almrei was moved to solitary confinement for his own protection before being transferred to the Millhaven Institution, a building that the government specifically built for individuals detained under security certificates.

Almrei's case involved a fundamental conflict between Canadian law and human rights. Under the security certificate, he was ordered deported to Syria. However, he faced the risk of arrest, torture and possible execution if he was sent back, because of his father's standing execution sentence. The government held him in custody for more than seven years, during which time he received plenty of support from members of Parliament and other notable figures willing to provide housing and put up sureties if the judge granted his release on bail. Although it was denied three times, Almrei's release was finally ordered by Federal Court Justice Richard Mosley on January 2, 2009. Almrei was to be strictly monitored, had to wear an electronic tracking bracelet and was ordered confined to his home.

Almost a year after Almrei's release, after having a security certificate against him dismissed by the Supreme Court of Canada then promptly re-issued, Mosley ruled on December 14, 2009, that, as Almrei had spent more than eight years in custody, the security certificate was no longer valid. While there might have been evidence in 2001 that made the certificate reasonable, Justice Mosley argued in a 183-page judgement that what evidence had seemed pertinent in 2001 no longer did in 2009. "While there were reasonable grounds to believe that Hassan Almrei was a danger to the security of Canada when he was detained in 2001, there are no longer reasonable grounds to believe that he is a security risk today."

Mosley's judgement was a slap in the face for CSIS. In it, he stated that the agency, "breached their duties of utmost good faith and candour to the court by not thoroughly reviewing the information in their possession, prior to the issuance of the February 2008 certificate." The statement from Mosley referred to the fact that an informant in the case had taken a lie detector test that found he was being deceptive with CSIS, while another informant had not taken a lie detector test, despite telling Mosley that he had. Mosley didn't know of the failed test.

Almrei may have spent the most time behind bars under a security certificate, but it was Mohammed Zeki Mahjoub who was the first person detained in the "war against terror," although his arrest predated the September 11 attacks.

Mahjoub was born and raised in Egypt, completed a university degree there and served in the military. He has stated that shortly after he left the army, he faced "persecution and torture" by the police because of his beliefs. After an attempt to leave the country was thwarted by the police, Mahjoub fled under the auspices of attending the annual Hajj pilgrimage, whereupon he travelled to Sudan and worked in agriculture. He personally met Osama bin Laden in Khartoum and took a job at his request overseeing one of his farms. Mahjoub left the position in 1993, claiming he was working too many hours for the amount of money he was making. On December 30, 1995, he came to Canada, gaining entry using a false Saudi Arabian passport he had purchased for $2500. For the first three weeks of his life in Toronto, he stayed with the family of Ahmed Said Khadr, a man who, along with other members of his family, was widely suspected of being involved in terrorism.

Mahjoub was granted refugee status in October 1996 because of his claim that his association with the Muslim Brotherhood in Egypt would likely lead to his arrest and torture. Once his refugee status was granted, Mahjoub began behaving strangely. He received numerous phone calls from Essam Marzouk, a member of the Vanguards of Conquest, a group devoted to the overthrow of the Egyptian government. Mahjoub was believed to be, along with Marzouk, a member of a violent splinter group of the Vanguards of Conquest known as al-Jihad. He later stated that he had no contact with Marzouk.

The two actually met at the Khadr household in 1998, and the phone calls continued. Mahjoub was again observed behaving in a suspicious nature as

CSIS watched him make a payphone call in December 1998. The watchers reported that Mahjoub had looked over his shoulder three times during the phone call. The Physical Surveillance Unit reported that Mahjoub always seemed to check over his shoulder, especially on one occasion when he got onto a bus after being at a local shopping mall.

CSIS interviewed Mahjoub six times between August 1997 and May 31, 1999, but the agency was not comfortable with the answers Mahjoub supplied and what the watchers had seen. In June 2000, CSIS secured the necessary signatures on the security certificate, at which point Mahjoub was detained. At the time of his arrest, he was carrying a piece of paper that listed Marzouk's former address.

A federal court judge ruled on October 5 that the certificate issued against Mahjoub was reasonable. The detainee also had the unenviable experience of contracting hepatitis C while incarcerated.

His detention became the source of some controversy. In January 2005, Judge Eleanor Dawson ruled that there was no evidence Mahjoub was a danger to Canada. His work on bin Laden's farm and his knowing the Khadr family—as did many in Toronto's Muslim community—were not sufficient evidence, she declared. A few months later, Mahjoub launched a hunger strike that lasted 76 days, living off liquids only and losing 110 pounds before he was hospitalized. With his health failing, and the risk he presented to Canada fading, the federal court on February 15, 2007, ordered his release, provided he wore a tracking bracelet. He was set free on April 12, 2007, but within a month he returned to the court and asked the judge to place him back in detention, claiming the surveillance requirements under which he was placed were a hardship on his family. Because he had not actually been charged with any crime, the judge could not grant Mahjoub's request.

When Mahjoub brought his request forward to the court again in March 2009, it was granted and he was imprisoned at Millhaven. Faced with what he claimed were poor conditions, including late food delivery, spilled milk, searches of his beard and even of his Koran by officials, Mahjoub began another hunger strike, this one lasting until he was again hospitalized in December 2009.

Justice Edward Blanchard maintained that there was little evidence before the court that would require Mahjoub to be kept in custody or to be subjected to the rigorous surveillance he had experienced earlier. In December 2009, one week after Mahjoub had been taken to hospital, the judge ruled that CSIS, the Crown and its witnesses "have adduced no independent evidence to support their position that a person of Mr. Mahjoub's background cannot change."

As of this writing, in a modified house-arrest release, Mahjoub lives alone in an apartment in Toronto, with a tracking bracelet affixed. His phone is tapped, he is under video surveillance, and voice-recognition software and motion detectors are installed inside his home. He is permitted to leave the apartment occasionally to run errands and to pray at a nearby mosque; federal agents have been ordered not to follow him during these times.

"I am satisfied that Mr. Mahjoub's lengthy detention has served to disrupt his contact and communication with extremist individuals or groups. I am also satisfied that the threat Mr. Mahjoub poses has been mitigated by his public exposure and by his constant supervision and control by the Canadian authorities," Blanchard stated.

The issue of Mahjoub's deportation has not yet been decided. He has been convicted in absentia in Egypt and sentenced to 15 years in prison. The leader of the Vanguards of Conquest, Kamel Agiza, a person whom CSIS has always contended Mahjoub was heavily involved with, conceded to Egyptian authorities in an interrogation—which many experts believe was conducted under torture—that Mahjoub was a member of al-Jihad. One judge and many of Mahjoub's supporters believe that he will be tortured or killed if he is deported to Egypt.

Mohammed Zeki Mahjoub is not the only individual in Canada detained under a security certificate for suspected involvement with al-Jihad. Mahmoud Es-Sayyid Jaballah, also an Egyptian in Canada, was detained on a certificate in August 2001 for association with the same group.

Jaballah was a frequent fixture in Egyptian police facilities following the assassination of former president Anwar Sadat, but the courts found him innocent of any involvement in the murder. The police arrested him later for membership in the student group al-Badr, but the courts once more declared him not guilty. Facing a lifetime of harassment by the Egyptian authorities, Jaballah left Egypt in 1991 and worked in Pakistan as a biology teacher and school principal, all under the auspices of the International Islamic Relief Organization, which has been declared sympathetic to al-Qaeda in some parts of the world.

He and his wife had six children before Jaballah applied as a refugee after entering Canada on May 11, 1996, on a false Saudi Arabian passport. Stamps on the passport indicated that the bearer had visited Pakistan 10 days before al-Jihad's attack on the Egyptian embassy there. Visits to Yemen, Azerbaijan, Jordan, Turkey and Germany, all in succession, were also denoted by the stamps.

Shortly after Jaballah arrived in Canada, CSIS maintains that he phoned other suspected members of al-Jihad, using code words the agency believed indicated the new refugee was trying to procure new travel documents. CSIS alleged that Jaballah had frequent contact with Ayman al-Zawahiri, the former leader of Egyptian Islamic Jihad, which al-Zawahiri eventually merged into al-Qaeda. Jaballah was associated with the Khadr family, as well as Mohammed Mahjoub.

Following Jaballah's series of arrests in London after the 1998 embassy bombings in Kenya and Tanzania, CSIS agents interviewed Jaballah. His phone records showed he had been in contact with each of the men arrested in London. Jaballah claimed not to recognize any of the names and refused to cooperate further. It was also noted that he had picked up several shipments of propaganda materials and allegedly received a fax in 1997 that offered helpful hints on how to recruit individuals for al-Jihad.

In 1999, Jaballah was arrested on a security certificate on the grounds that he was a prominent member of the terrorist group al-Jihad. The initial review of the security certificate found the evidence did not support the charges, and he was released after several months. His freedom lasted until August 2001, when he was detained on a second certificate on the same grounds. He was kept in the Toronto West Detention Centre until he, like all the other men arrested on security certificates, was transferred to Millhaven in 2006.

In April 2007, Jaballah was released from custody and escorted to the family home where he was outfitted with a tracking bracelet. He cannot have unauthorized visitors, cannot leave the residence without approval and must have all his mail opened and phone calls recorded. He is also not allowed to use a cell phone or have an Internet connection. The courts have not yet settled the issue of his deportation as he likely faces retribution from Egyptian authorities.

It is difficult to concede that the man pumping your gas could possibly be a terrorist intent on ending your life, but that's exactly what CSIS was arguing when it issued a security certificate against Mohamed Harkat in December 2002.

Harkat was raised in Algeria and studied at the University of Oran. In 1989, he joined an association known as the Front Islamique du Salut (FIS), a political party that at the time was considered a legitimate Islamic political party. He allowed FIS members to use the family house as a registered district office. In March 1990, the Algerian government, suspicious of the party's activities, raided the home and arrested everyone inside. Harkat was not there at the time, but an uncle warned him about the raids, and Harkat fled for Saudi Arabia. He flew to Pakistan where he found work with the Muslim World League that used him in the Peshawar district to hand out relief packages and organize aid programs. During that time, CSIS alleges that Harkat worked for a group called Human Concern International, an organization in which Ahmed Said Khadr was once heavily involved. CSIS also alleges that Harkat ran a guest house for foreign *mujahideen* who were travelling to fight in the civil war in Afghanistan.

After losing his job in 1994, Harkat joined Groupe Islamique Armé, the more militant wing of the FIS. He spent time in Malaysia, purchased a forged Saudi passport and caught a flight to Toronto to make a refugee claim. He stayed at the home of a friend with whom he had associated at the World Muslim League. After claiming that he would likely be persecuted for his membership in FIS if he returned to Algeria, his refugee claim was granted, and he applied for permanent residency.

CSIS, however, was already suspicious of Harkat, accusing him of using an alias "Abu Muslima," which he subsequently denied. He soon developed a gambling problem and lost thousands of dollars at local casinos. He got a job pumping gas, as well as delivering pizza, and eventually married a Canadian woman named Sophie Lamarche.

On December 10, 2002, officials detained Harkat on a security certificate that, according to secret evidence obtained by CSIS, stated Harkat was a threat to national security. The agency had a statement from a U.S. source that said a man resembling Harkat had run a guest house in Pakistan designed to shuttle fighters to Chechnya. The security certificate was upheld as reasonable in 2005, and Harkat was moved to the Millhaven Institution in April 2006. On May 23 of that year, federal court justice Eleanor Dawson finally released him on a $100,000 surety. Under his release, Harkat had to be in the company of either his wife or mother-in-law at all times and had to wear a tracking bracelet. He was prohibited from using any form of electronic communication, and the Canada Border Services Agency had to approve any trips outside his house, during which he was to be accompanied by two agents.

Harkat, however, appealed the case of his certificate to the Supreme Court of Canada, which would rule on the issue of the constitutionality of security certificates as a whole. While on release, he was arrested for breaching the conditions of the security certificate when he was found alone at home after his mother-in-law had left because of a fight with her husband. Harkat was later released without charge. The Supreme Court ruled in his favour, striking down the constitutionality of security certificates but giving the government a year to draft new legislation. New security certificates were subsequently ordered for all of the men detained under them.

At a hearing in 2008, Judge Simon Noel ruled that CSIS had to disclose its secret evidence to Harkat and that his legal team must have the opportunity to review it. Noel amended Harkat's release conditions, too, to allow him to remain home alone without his wife or mother-in-law present. By May 2009, Noel was starting to get irritated with CSIS, in part because he had received information that two of the witnesses from CSIS might have lied about the reliability of a key informant in the case. Noel wondered if CSIS had deliberately misled the court as he had repeatedly asked the agency about the informant's reliability. As a result, Noel ordered the Crown to make a top-secret file available to Harkat's two special advisors that included the name of the informant.

"The rule of law requires no less," Noel said.

On June 6, 2009, CSIS revealed that its key informant in the Harkat case had failed a lie detector test. The test, administered in 2002, demonstrated that the man was being truthful when questioned about his interactions with other agencies but was being untruthful when other "relevant questions" were asked.

On October 21, 2009, Noel ordered another secret file be made available to Harkat's advocates and ruled that, in his opinion, CSIS had not been deliberately trying to mislead him when they failed to inform him of the failed polygraph test.

On February 2, 2010, Harkat took the stand in his own defence in a federal court in Toronto and denied having run a guest house in the Peshawar region, as well as ever having met or worked for Ahmed Khadr, a former Canadian associate of Osama bin Laden and a well-known fundraiser for terrorist movements originating out of Afghanistan.

"Your honour, I never worked for Khadr or went in his office [in Peshawar]," Harkat told Noel. As for a Peshawar safe house, it "never happened," said Harkat.

Now 41 years old, Harkat has described the "nightmare" of being forced to flee his native Algeria because of his association with FIS. As of this writing, Harkat's hearings are scheduled to continue.

Adil Charkaoui's practise of karate and such pursuits was one of the reasons that the Moroccan-born man who came to Canada in 1973 was viewed as a deadly terrorist threat.

Charkaoui moved with his parents and sisters to Montréal, where he attended university and received a master's degree. He later found work as a French teacher. Three years after coming to Canada, Charkaoui left for Pakistan to study religion. At this time, it is

INTELLIGENCE SHIFT   179

alleged he travelled from Pakistan to Afghanistan and
attended a terrorist training camp under an alias. The
Canadian government asserted that, between 1992
and the end of the millennium, Charkaoui could not
be accounted for.

When the government issued a security certificate
against Charkaoui in May 2003, it asserted that while
allegedly attending the Afghan training camp, he was
most likely trained in the use of "operating rocket-
propelled grenade-launchers, sabotage, urban combat
and assassination." One argument, seemingly foolish at
face value, said, "it was noteworthy that one of those
who participated in the hijacking of [the September 11
attacks] had taken martial arts training in preparation."
In the government's opinion, Charkaoui's admission to
studying karate and his past travels indicated that he
was a sleeper agent who needed to be detained and
deported to his native Morocco.

After being taken into custody without charge and
later freed on $50,000 bail in 2005, Charkaoui, who
always denied the government's claims against him,
appealed his case all the way to the Supreme Court of
Canada. The landmark decision struck down the
legitimacy of security certificates because they
infringed on several sections of the Canadian Charter
of Rights and Freedoms, but the court suspended its
judgement for one year in order to allow the government of the day to create new legislation.

One of most significant pieces of evidence against
Charkaoui that supported the government's theory
that he had attended a terrorist training camp came

from the "Millennium Bomber," Ahmed Ressam. As Ressam awaited sentencing in his case for trying to bomb the Los Angeles airport, he had initially helped police forces, with the understanding he might receive a more lenient sentence. Ressam had provided information against two Montréalers, one of whom was Charkaoui. Ressam testified that he had seen Charkaoui at a terrorist training camp in Afghanistan. However, after suffering what the media has described as a "mental breakdown" in prison, Ressam stopped co-operating with authorities and later recanted much of the evidence he had given.

A newspaper reporter in Montréal wrote to Ressam after the would-be terrorist had recanted his evidence against one Montréaler and asked if he still maintained that he had seen Charkaoui in Afghanistan. Ressam responded in a letter that he was recanting all of the evidence he had given against him. Ressam claimed that, at the time of his interrogation by CSIS agents, he had been "psychologically unbalanced."

Ressam's recantation led to some, but not much, doubt about the case against Charkaoui. Several news articles citing evidence from the government's case stated that, among other activities, Charkaoui was serving as a recruiter, looking for people to fight in jihad prior to September 11, appearing at "nerve centres" such as mosques and inviting people to meetings, then interviewing them to determine if they had any security issues in their backgrounds that would make them unsuitable. His associates painted him in a negative light. Regardless of his recanted association with Ressam, Charkaoui was friends with another suspected terrorist. A newspaper article detailing the relationship stated that the pair was once heard discussing a plot to hijack a commercial jetliner in June 2000.

But in 2008, the case started to turn in Charkaoui's favour. After it was admitted in court that CSIS had destroyed much of the evidence against him, especially recordings of interviews with him, the Supreme Court of Canada ruled that "CSIS should be required to retain all the information in its possession." In February 2009, a federal court justice ordered the release of Charkaoui's bail terms, stating that the danger he once posed was "neutralized by the passage of time." His 10:00 PM curfew was lifted, he could own a cell phone and have Internet access, he was free to leave his house alone, and he could leave Montréal after giving the authorities 48 hours' notice of his intention to do so. But he still had to wear a tracking bracelet.

Judge Daniele Tremblay-Lamer had already ruled that some of the government's "secret" information against Charkaoui could be released to him and his special advocates without endangering national security. That information included files on wiretaps, the human sources against him and intelligence services. When Tremblay-Lamer reiterated her stance in September 2009, the government, unwilling to oblige, withdrew its information against Charkaoui instead of proceeding with the case.

With the evidence withdrawn, Tremblay-Lamer ruled that there was nothing to support the justification of the security certificate and immediately lifted it, as well as Charkaoui's bail conditions. He was permitted to remove his monitoring bracelet and leave the courthouse a free man. CSIS stood by the accuracy of its information and launched an appeal before Tremblay-Lamer, asking her to reconsider, but the judge ruled that none of the "new" evidence filed with the court warranted reversing her decision.

"It is worth noting to what point the notion of national security is a question of perspective. Grey areas can exist where a misunderstanding is possible," Tremblay-Lamer ruled.

Within months of the decision, Charkaoui was threatening to sue the government. While incarcerated, he stated, he missed the birth of one of his children and had been labelled a terrorist.

"I hope [the government] will be reasonable and apologize," Charkaoui stated. No such apology has been made, and the chances of one being issued are quite small.

Adil Charkaoui's was the last case in which a security certificate had been issued for a suspected terrorist. None have been executed since his detention in 2003. However, other individuals linked to Canada have ended up in trouble with the authorities based on information either collected by Canada or misinterpreted by another agency.

In 1994, Mohammed Mansour Jabarah came to Canada from Kuwait at the age of 12 with the hope of eventually becoming an ophthalmologist. His father opened a gas station in St. Catharines, Ontario, where the family had settled. Every summer, Jabarah and his brother travelled back to Kuwait to stay with relatives. Chief among their friends was an Islamic instructor by the name of Sulaiman Abu Ghaith, a man who later joined al-Qaeda. Soon Jabarah fell under the sway of the powerful terrorist organization, going so far as to meet its leader, Osama bin Laden, one summer. When Jabarah returned to Canada after one of his visits to Kuwait, he started fundraising, and he passed the proceeds to individuals to help fuel the war in Chechnya, where many Muslims were fighting against the Russians.

Jabarah attended his first Afghan terror training camp in the summer of 2000, a 10-week program at Al Farouq. After completing the course and vowing his allegiance to bin Laden, Jabarah turned down an offer from the camp to become an instructor and instead travelled to Karachi, Pakistan. Shortly after the 9/11 attacks, he left Pakistan for Hong Kong, and then Kuala Lumpur, Malaysia, where he met with militants at a local fast-food chain. He went to Singapore and met with two other individuals to start planning an attack against several embassies there. An al-Qaeda agent passed him $10,000 to give to local militants.

However, before the plan to attack the embassies in Singapore could be carried out, police moved in on the local militant group, and Jabarah fled back to the

Middle East, first to Dubai in 2002 and then to Oman. In March 2002, the authorities in Oman arrested him because he had been cited as a wanted terrorist. Instead of passing him over to the Americans, Oman contacted CSIS, who sent two agents to pick him up and take him back to Canada.

Once they had him back in Canada, CSIS interrogated Jabarah for four straight days. With Jabarah offering little in the way of information, CSIS devised a ploy in which an agent who had befriended him at a strip club in Toronto stated the Americans were interested in talking to him for just a few hours. It was a complete fabrication. The Americans took Jabarah into custody, but he was released to a series of safe houses to work as a double agent after agreeing to cooperate with the Americans.

When members of the FBI searched Jabarah's house, they turned up a "hit list" of American agents and prosecutors, a knife and rope and bomb-making instructions. Devotional notes to bin Laden were also found, as well as other documents supportive of the actions of the September 11 hijackers. Jabarah was promptly jailed in New York City. Any hope he had that the authorities would look kindly on his cooperation was destroyed by the presiding judge in his case. Stating that Jabarah's actions spoke for themselves, Judge Barbara S. Jones promptly slapped Jabarah with a life sentence.

The actions of CSIS in the case, however, drew the ire of many, including the Canadian Civil Liberties Association (which ruled that CSIS had violated

Jabarah's Charter rights) and the Security Intelligence Review Committee. In 2007, SIRC released a report blasting the intelligence service's actions. It stated that the agency had created the apprehension of detention, had not advised Jabarah of his right to stay silent or his right to be represented by a lawyer, all serious Charter violations.

Jabarah is currently serving his life sentence in the United States. In April 2009, he had launched a hunger strike that came to public light in June of that year. His health became such a concern that doctors eventually force-fed him through a tube inserted into his nose. According to his family, Jabarah was protesting that the authorities had placed heavy restrictions on his mail for 41 months, sometimes withholding mail from his family, including a copy of the Koran. His father, Mansour, told the press that his son simply wanted to be able to phone his family and attend Sunday prayers.

Born in the Sudan in the 1960s, Abousfian Abdelrazik became a Canadian citizen in 1995. When he left Canada in 2003 in the company of his wife and children to visit his mother, Abdelrazik did not anticipate the six years of terror and dread that he would face.

After his wife and children returned to Canada, Abdelrazik was arrested by the Sudanese authorities and allegedly tortured. After he was released in the spring of 2004, Abdelrazik was informed that he could not travel because his name had been placed, at the request of the United States, on the United Nations no-fly list. In 2005, the Sudanese police again arrested Abdelrazik, this time releasing him in July 2006. According to parts of a heavily redacted Department of Foreign Affairs and International Trade (DFAIT) document that Abdelrazik's lawyer later used in court, he might have been apprehended in the Sudan at the request of CSIS. The agency later denied the claim, and its director ordered a full review of the case.

Abdelrazik's passport had expired while in custody, but the Canadian government refused to grant him a new one. He spent more than a year living inside the Canadian embassy as supporters in Canada rallied the government to support him and bring him home. Abdelrazik launched a legal challenge, claiming that his Charter rights to "enter, remain in and leave Canada" were being denied and asking the court to order his return.

Several sympathetic individuals donated money to purchase a plane ticket back to Canada for him, but the government still refused to issue him a new passport. According to the government, even if Canada did allow Abdelrazik to get onto a plane, the country would be in violation of the UN no-fly list because he would be forced to fly through countries that did not want him in their airspace.

Abdelrazik's supporters started making more allegations concerning his detention, one of which stated that a Canadian diplomat had advised embassy staff in the Sudan "not to accompany Abdelrazik to his interview" with Sudanese intelligence agents. Abdelrazik later asserted that CSIS had sent agents to interrogate him while he was in prison. CSIS, however, refuted the allegations, stating instead that Abdelrazik's presence on the no-fly list had been requested by the American government and that CSIS did not know what evidence the Americans had. CSIS had been watching Abdelrazik years earlier because of his ties with other suspect individuals.

On June 4, 2009, a federal court ordered the government to repatriate Abdelrazik within 30 days' time. Two weeks later, the government announced that it would fly Abdelrazik home after issuing him a temporary set of travel documents. Fourteen days afterward, Abdelrazik landed in Canada, with 50 supporters and a brass band waiting for him in Montréal when his plane landed.

"I am happy to be home," was all he said as he was ushered away.

Both CSIS and the RCMP stated they have no evidence that Abdelrazik was involved in terrorist activities. A month after his return, he called on the government to remove his name from the UN no-fly list, which he claimed led to his assets being frozen and his difficulty finding a job or getting health insurance. SIRC has promised a full investigation into the matter of his detention. Abdelrazik has launched a lawsuit against the government.

Of all of the cases that emerged after the horrific attacks of September 11, 2001, none generated more publicity than that of Maher Arar, a telecommunications engineer who was born in Syria and moved to Canada at the age of 17. Although his supporters were quick to blame CSIS for his deportation and torture, a commission of inquiry later determined that CSIS played a very minor part.

In September 2002, Arar, then age 32, was coming back to Canada after a holiday with his family in Tunis. During a stopover in New York City, Arar was taken into custody by Immigration and Naturalization Service (INS) officials at the airport and interrogated. Unfortunately for Arar, because he held citizenship in both Canada and Syria, and the U.S. somehow believed he might be involved in terrorism, the United States invoked its policy of "extraordinary rendition." After two weeks of interrogation and claims that he was a member of al-Qaeda, Arar was shipped to Syria where he was promptly taken into custody. What followed, Arar later described, was horrific.

"They made me bend my head down in the back seat," Arar said of being blindfolded once he arrived in Amman, Jordan, his first stop on the way to Syria. "Then these men started beating me. Every time I tried to talk, they beat me."

The beatings continued for several hours until Arar told the interrogators what they wanted to hear—that he was a member of al-Qaeda and had attended one of their training camps in Afghanistan. From that point on, he was imprisoned in a 1 x 2 metre cell infested with rats, held in solitary confinement and beaten regularly with cables. In October 2003, after Syrian authorities stated that they could find no links between Arar and al-Qaeda, Arar was released and returned to Canada. He immediately began a legal challenge in both Canada and the United States to clear his name. The RCMP announced it would investigate the circumstances of his arrest and rendition.

In reality, Arar had been the subject of some initial CSIS-RCMP surveillance dating back to the late 1990s. Project A-O Canada was a joint task force created in response to the presence of several persons of interest in Canada. Warranting particular attention was a man named Abdullah Almalki, who had been under surveillance because of his associations with Ahmed Khadr. However, when the American authorities contacted the RCMP about Arar after his arrest in 2002, the prominence of Arar in that project, while downplayed by CSIS, was ramped up by the RCMP. The preliminary RCMP report concluded that the RCMP had shared sensitive information on Arar without first determining how it would be used. There were some hints that an officer involved might have known the United States was going to use the information to deport Arar to Syria, but he never shared that information with his superiors.

On February 5, 2004, the government established the Commission of Inquiry into the Actions of Canadian Officials in Relation to Maher Arar. The commission heard from 85 witnesses, including Canada's former ambassador to Syria, who evoked outrage and incredulity across the country when he told the commission that he had no reason to believe Arar was being mistreated and that, to the best of his knowledge, the Syrians seldom engaged in such activity. The believability of his testimony was damaged by Syria's well-known reputation for infringing on fundamental human rights.

Justice Dennis O'Connor, who oversaw the commission, issued his final report in September 2006, in which he stated "there is no evidence to indicate that Mr. Arar has committed any offence or that his activities constitute a threat to the security of Canada." O'Connor stated that he believed Arar was tortured, and that the RCMP's decision to share sensitive, inaccurate information with the American authorities had been wrong. Both the Mounties and the government later apologized to Arar. He received $11.5 million in compensation.

CHAPTER TEN

Family or Foes?

OF PARTICULAR INTEREST TO CSIS, prior to and especially following the attacks of September 11, 2001, was an Ontario family long rumoured to have links to terrorist groups overseas.

Ahmed Said Khadr moved to Canada in 1975 from Egypt. After spending a few months in Montréal, he enrolled at the University of Ottawa to study computer programming. While helping out at Camp Al-Mu-Mee-Neen near Creemore, Ontario, Khadr met Maha Elsamnah, with whom he immediately fell in love. The pair married at a Toronto mosque. In 1979, the couple gave birth to their first child, Zaynab. It was during this time that Khadr began to demonstrate some of the religious devotion that later brought him under the watch of CSIS.

Khadr joined the Muslim Students Association, became a supporter of *sharia* and a vocal advocate for Islamic rule in Egypt. Disenchanted with the decadent lifestyle of the West, Khadr and his family moved to Bahrain where he was offered a position as a professor at a university. The couple welcomed a son, Abdullah, in 1981, and second son—Abdurahman—

followed in 1982, but his birth was overshadowed by the Soviet invasion of Afghanistan. Khadr's supporters have said it was only his devotion to help the poor and not the resistance effort that compelled him to travel to Pakistan to join a Kuwaiti relief organization called Lajnat al-Da'wa. Khadr's work led to a great deal of recognition, so much so that he was often referred to as "al-Kanadi," or "the Canadian."

The family returned to Canada several times a year where Khadr engaged in fundraising activities for the charitable group. While in Pakistan, a jumping-off point for many of the *mujahideen* travelling from across the world to fight the Soviets, Khadr came to know many of the fighters personally. He met Ayman al-Zawahiri, an important figure in the movement and a known arms dealer working in the refugee camps. Khadr is alleged to have also met Osama bin Laden.

Unfortunately, all was not well on the family front. Khadr's second youngest son, Ibrahim, had been born with a congenital heart defect and was eventually sent back to Canada to stay with his grandparents for treatment. In 1988, Ibrahim fell ill and died, despite being rushed to hospital.

Khadr, however, was on the move, now working with Human Concern International, a Canadian charity group operating in Peshawar. But the charity was tainted by the touch of Osama bin Laden, who had linked himself and his activities with the society in a media interview. Khadr was now under suspicion as a moneyman, someone who worked for the charity but distributed money to groups in Afghanistan from Pakistan. These reports were later verified by members of the Chinese intelligence community and cited in CSIS documents as the reason for its subsequent investigation. Khadr changed jobs from Human Concern to a group affiliated with the Muslim World League. He stated that the people living in the north of the country were lacking in care while there were many non-governmental organizations (NGOs) in the West helping out.

Khadr's time in Afghanistan was cut short in 1992, however, because of a severe shrapnel injury he received, the cause of which has been disputed. According to Human Concern International, Khadr was injured when he stepped on a landmine inside one of the refugee camps. His son Abdurahman later stated he was injured by a bomb in a pitched battle between two warlords. With the medical care in Pakistan unable to treat Khadr's punctured bladder and kidney, he returned to Toronto for treatment where doctors were able to successfully stitch him back together.

After a long convalescence, Khadr returned to Pakistan to continue his work but knocked heads with other managers after his long leave. His family claimed that the despair he felt at the situation in Afghanistan, especially the ongoing fighting between regional warlords throughout the country, led him to radicalize his children. He taught them of the nobility and promised rewards that came from martyrdom and self-sacrifice. In 1994, he dispatched his two oldest sons—Abdurahman and Abdullah— to the Khalden training camp.

The entire family soon fell under the suspicion of Pakistani authorities after Khadr's daughter's fiancé was implicated as a suspect in the 1995 bombing of the Egyptian embassy in Pakistan that killed 17 people. At the time, however, Khadr was in Afghanistan, and his family, who were at their home in Pakistan, were all taken into custody. Authorities who searched the home found almost $80,000 in cash—Khadr said it was for his workers, but it was later stated that he was laundering the money to finance the attack on the embassy.

Khadr returned to Pakistan and was subsequently arrested and imprisoned for his role in the attack. When Prime Minister Jean Chrétien visited Pakistan in 1996, the government asked the Pakistanis about Khadr's status. Chrétien spoke directly to Pakistani prime minister Benazir Bhutto, who replied Khadr was being treated well. The government soon dropped the charges for lack of evidence and set Khadr free. The Khadrs quickly returned to Canada.

The authorities with the Canadian International Development Agency (CIDA), responsible for co-ordinating overseas aid, was already aware of Khadr's arrest and went directly to CSIS for advice. As a result of Khadr's arrest and the alleged link between Osama bin Laden and Human Concern International, CIDA responded by cancelling funding to the organization.

Anyone associating with the Khadrs soon came under suspicion by CSIS agents keeping tabs on local suspected terrorist group members. Mohammed Zeki Mahjoub and Mahmoud Jaballah—both of whom ended up being arrested on security certificates—met the Khadr family on several different occasions, sharing tea and meeting Khadr's in-laws. Khadr met with Mohammad Harkat in Ottawa, although the extent to which they actually knew one another was eventually disputed.

Pakistan later stated it did in fact believe Khadr had played a role in the Egyptian embassy attack and that he might have been involved in the 1998 bombings of the U.S. embassies in Kenya and Tanzania. Khadr, however, could not be found. He was rumoured to have travelled back to either Pakistan or Afghanistan, where he met with Osama bin Laden.

With Khadr's reputation preceding him, England added his name to a United Nations' list of individuals believed to finance terrorism. Following the 2001 terrorist attacks, the list was amended to include his association with Osama bin Laden. As a result, no member of the United Nations was permitted to engage in any kind of commerce with Khadr.

Great Britain wasn't the only country who believed that Khadr was a key terrorist supporter. Following 9/11, the United States added his name to a list of individuals wanted in connection with the attacks and promptly froze all of his assets.

Yet in all of this, as CSIS watched Khadr, the Canadian government refused to take action. Khadr's prominence as someone associated with terrorism made it into the House of Commons. Conservative MP Brian Pallister asked the government, given that the United States and the United

Kingdom were taking steps against Khadr, "Why has this government not frozen the assets of either of his organizations?" Pallister was referring to Human Concern International and Khadr's own Toronto-based Health and Education Project International.

It turned out the Khadrs were in Afghanistan and had managed to flee from Kabul one day before the Northern Alliance—now backed by the Allied nations of the West—captured the city from the Taliban. In January 2002, the RCMP raided the family's Canadian property where it found some questionable evidence, mainly a photograph of Khadr standing with a *muja-hid* beside an anti-aircraft gun.

Slowly but surely, the Khadr family began to emerge, but Ahmed was nowhere to be found. In November 2002, Abdurahman was captured by the Northern Alliance. Khadr and another son, Abdullah, were dispatched to the Pakistan-Afghanistan border to help organize militants arriving to fight back against the armies of the West. Abdullah was charged with looking for weapons. Abdullah later returned to Canada and made himself available to the media after a rumour surfaced that he had been a suicide bomber who killed a Canadian solider in 2004.

"If I was the suicide bomber, I wouldn't be doing this interview with you right now," he told the media on February 25, 2004.

Accused of running al-Qaeda terrorist training camps, which he subsequently denied, Abdullah was arrested in Pakistan then sent back to Canada. At the request of U.S. authorities, he was arrested in Toronto on December 7, 2005, and later indicted in Massachusetts on February 8, 2006, on charges of conspiring to kill American soldiers in Afghanistan, conspiracy to use weapons of mass destruction and conspiracy to possess a destructive device to commit violent crimes. He was held without bail. His grandmother offered to put up her home as a surety to secure his bail, but the judge hearing the case refused, stating "I do not trust Mr. Khadr, nor do I trust his grandmother."

His extradition hearing is scheduled to take place in April 2010.

Zaynab Khadr, the family's only daughter, also fell under suspicion of the authorities, even as she became one of her family's most ardent defenders. It was her engagement that led to her father's initial arrest in Afghanistan and the subsequent notoriety of the Khadr name worldwide. After being married twice and giving birth to a boy, she returned to Canada from Pakistan in February 2005, although the Canadian High Commission in Pakistan had revoked her passport. When she arrived in Canada, security officials were waiting for her with a warrant, stating that she "has willingly participated and contributed both directly and indirectly towards enhancing the ability of al-Qaeda."

The agents promptly seized her laptop, several DVDs, tapes, a diary and a bundle of files. She was, however, never charged, and she asserted that she had purchased the computer second-hand. Zaynab later appeared in a documentary entitled *Son of al Qaeda*, in which she spoke about the September 11 attacks and stated that it wasn't pleasant to watch people being killed, "But you just sort of think, 'They deserve it. They've been doing it for such a long time. Why shouldn't they feel it once in a while?'"

The media immediately seized on the comments, making her out to be a supporter of the 9/11 hijackers. Zaynab lives in Canada, unable to leave because the government will not issue her a new passport. She has taken up an advocacy role to help individuals imprisoned because of association with terrorism. In October 2008, she climbed Parliament Hill and began an 18-day hunger strike to draw attention to government inaction with respect to certain members of her family.

Unlike some other members of his family, Ahmed Khadr elected to stay in Pakistan, a decision that would cost him his life. On October 2, 2003, Ahmed, his son Abdulkareem and several others were staying at a safe house in a village in South Waziristan, when a rumour began to spread that a Pakistani raid was on the way. The next day, despite making attempts to try to leave the village, they were still there when helicopters and hundreds of troops arrived. According to some, Abdulkareem was shot in the spine when he tried to take cover in a ditch in the ensuing battle; he was left a paraplegic. Other stories claim an Unmanned Aerial Vehicle (UAV)—an American Predator drone—had attacked the safe house. Several others were arrested at the scene, but for the longest time, no one knew what had happened to Ahmed. The government released a list of dead to the media, but his name was not on it, and Pakistani officials reported that Abdulkareem had been unable to identify his father from photographs of the dead and wounded.

An attorney, hired by Maha Khadr, Ahmed's wife, asked the Supreme Court of Pakistan to submit details about the status of both her son and husband. It took until January 2004 for Pakistan to confirm, via DNA, that Ahmed had died in the battle, his body found outside the doorway to the safe house. Some media in the area claimed that Khadr had been killed in January after another raid in the Pakistani town of Wana. A CSIS source, however, testified in federal court that Ahmed had died in 2004. The outcome was that he was deemed to have been killed in October 2003.

The Northern Alliance captured Abdurahman, and he was jailed at Camp X-Ray at Guantanamo Bay. He said he was trained as a CIA undercover operative. After being bounced from country to country, he was finally allowed to return to Canada in 2003, where he held a press conference. The media reported he had been released because he had divulged the location of his father, a charge Abdurahman steadfastly denied. In March 2004, however, he granted three interviews to PBS in which he claimed that his family was an "al-Qaeda family" and that he resented his father for associating with militants.

Numerous contradictions in his stories, however, led him to admit that he had told several lies, not including his comments to PBS. The government has repeatedly denied him a passport under the "royal prerogative," where the Queen (or by extension, the Governor General) can act, based on common law and authority, upon the government's advice. The government resorted to the tactic when it turned out that being a threat to national security was not sufficient grounds to withhold a passport from a Canadian citizen, hence the use of the royal prerogative.

Ahmed Khadr continued to make headlines after his death. While hearing the government's case in issuing a security certificate for the deportation of Mohamed Harkat, a federal court judge ruled that Ahmed Khadr had provided prospective terrorist recruits entry to Afghanistan's terrorist camps. His links to bin Laden were considered so strong that Khadr became a "reference" for would-be fighters, writing letters to the administrators of terrorist camps overseas vouching for individuals who wished to go there for training. It was another blow to the Khadr family that was reeling from a sustained attack on both their reputation and their family.

The patriarch of the Khadr family was dead, and one of their sons had lost the use of his legs. Another son was in jail, awaiting extradition and another had essentially cut off ties with the family and was now declaring them to be a group of terrorists. And yet there was still more controversy and conflict to come.

Omar Khadr was the fifth of the Khadrs' children, remembered as a bright and polite young man during the time he spent in Canada. Like all of the other Khadrs, he was frequently shuttled from Canada to Pakistan or Afghanistan, especially after his father's arrest. Following an incident in Afghanistan in which Omar was forced to dress as a girl to disguise himself, an act that made him angry, he asked his father for permission to live at a group home for young men. One month later, he joined a group of men in need of a Pashto translator. Although he promised to check in at home as often as he could, his visits became less and less frequent as Omar learned about becoming a fighter, receiving one-on-one weapons training. He eventually accompanied the men to a village to meet with several other militants.

On the morning of July 27, 2002, a group of American Special Forces, infantry and Afghan militia left their outpost at Khost to investigate a local villager who was alleged to be a bomb maker. As they searched the man's home, they received a report that a satellite phone had just been used within only a few hundred metres of their position. One squad set off to have a look, arriving at a collection of mud huts and a granary. After noticing some men sitting around a fire in a residence with AK-47 automatic rifles nearby, the squad called for support, then approached the house. A man sleeping under a nearby tree woke up and yelled. The militiamen were sent in to translate, as well as to request the surrender of the five men inside the house. More infantry arrived to reinforce the American team, making for a total of 50 soldiers.

When the men inside the hut heard that the Americans wanted to search the residence, they grabbed their guns and opened fire. Several grenades were lobbed in the direction of the team. Three soldiers were wounded and dragged away from the fight, prompting a call for a medical evacuation. Two transport helicopters from the 57th Medical Detachment and two AH-64 Apache gunships responded. A pair of F-18 Hornet fighters lobbed several bombs onto the house. They were replaced by a flight of A-10 Warthog planes that attacked other houses. With the medical helicopters gone and the house largely in ruins, a squad was dispatched to examine the interior.

Unbeknownst to the squad, one militiaman and another young man had survived the bombing and firefight. Suddenly a grenade was thrown out of the house, and it detonated near Sergeant Christopher Speer, a Delta Force member who was not wearing a helmet. One of the men in the home emerged, and he was promptly shot in the head.

Another young man was found in the rubble, his eye bleeding from a shrapnel wound. He was shot twice in the back, the bullets penetrating his body and passing through his chest. The young man received on-site medical attention despite his repeated requests for the soldiers to kill him, which, according to the diary of an officer on scene, almost happened until a Delta Force soldier intervened. The young man was loaded aboard a transport helicopter and flown to Bagram Airbase.

Sergeant Speer was flown to Ramstein Air Base in Germany, where the United States military maintains a world-class hospital, but his injuries proved too serious. He was subsequently removed from life support on August 7, 2002, and all his usable organs were donated.

A search of the house the day after the attack revealed a hidden underground chamber that contained ammunition, rockets, grenades and rocket-propelled grenades. There were also wires, documents, and a videocassette. The young man shot in the gun battle was on the video—he was seen manipulating detonator cord as other men in the home assembled explosives.

Meanwhile, the same young man was recovering from his wounds and was being interrogated by officials. He identified himself as Omar Khadr, a Canadian citizen. He was weak and still suffering from injuries to his eye—other detainees later testified that U.S. officials denied Khadr surgery that would have saved his vision because he did not give the interrogators the information they were looking for. A pair of sunglasses to protect his eyesight was also forbidden for "state security" reasons.

Two weeks after Speer died, the United States finally informed Canada they had captured Omar and were trying to confirm his identity. Within 10 days, the Canadian government responded, requesting access to its citizen, which was subsequently refused another 10 days later. U.S. officials said they would only notify Canada if the prisoner was moved to Camp X-Ray at Guantanamo Bay, Cuba.

In evidence later released to the public, Omar stated that the Americans refused him pain medication, tied his hands above a door frame, doused him in cold water, threatened him with dogs and forced him to endure several soldiers passing gas on him. As it turned out, the same man in charge of Omar's interrogation pleaded guilty to abusing detainees in the case of an in-custody death.

Canada sent a letter asking the Americans not to transfer Omar to Guantanamo Bay and to keep in mind the delicate relationship between the two countries, but the interrogation continued. Omar allegedly told his interrogators he had fought to defend Islam and that, having heard of a $1500 bounty placed on the head of every American soldier killed, stated, "I wanted to kill a lot of Americans to get lots of money."

What the Americans chose to ignore at the time of Omar's capture was that he was only 15 years old, qualifying him as a child soldier and eligible to special treatment under the conventions governing the treatment of prisoners of war. The United States argued that because Omar was not a member of an actual army, and therefore was not technically a soldier, he was lumped in, as with all the other Taliban members captured, as an "unlawful enemy combatant" and afforded no protection under the conventions.

(It is interesting to note that Omar was presented with a picture of Maher Arar. He first said that he didn't recognize him, then later stated he had seen him at a Kabul safe house. The following day, Arar was sent to Syria.)

After three months at Bagram, where he was used as a labourer and called a murderer, Omar was transferred to Guantanamo. Despite the earlier promise, the Canadian government was not notified of the move. Facing charges of terrorism and war crimes,

Omar was treated as an adult prisoner despite his youth. American intelligence officials were excited about Omar's presence, hoping he could provide information on the whereabouts of his father and a list of who's who of al-Qaeda, given that he had met its leader, Osama bin Laden (Omar had been 10 years old at the time).

The Canadian government was finally notified of Khadr's transfer, and in February 2003, an intelligence officer from the Department of Foreign Affairs and a CSIS agent flew to Cuba to interrogate Omar. During the three weeks before the Canadians arrived, Omar was awakened every three hours and moved to a new cell in an effort to make him more receptive to interrogation. The Canadians, under the auspices of ascertaining his well-being, arrived with a Big Mac meal from McDonald's. What emerged was a summary that described Omar as a "thoroughly screwed up young man."

When Omar's Canadian lawyers learned of the visit and five more in 2003–04, they were granted a federal court injunction by an Edmonton judge that barred any member of CSIS from interrogating him again. CSIS was criticized because it had shared what it had learned with the Americans, who were intent on prosecuting Omar at Guantanamo. Assistant director of CSIS William Hooper later stated the goal of the interrogation was not to provide the Americans with evidence for the prosecution. He admitted that all the information CSIS had extracted from Omar had been shared with their American cousins without any sort of guarantee, such as ruling out the death penalty.

Khadr's subsequent treatment in prison was deplorable. He was repeatedly threatened with torture, rendition to another country and anal rape. He was also spat on, had his hair pulled out and was left shackled in awkward positions until he soiled himself. And, on one occasion, he was dragged on the floor in a solution of his own urine and pine oil, then not permitted to change clothes for two days.

After a meeting with his lawyers, who later determined that Omar was suffering from delusions and hallucinations, suicidal behaviour and "intense paranoia," Omar was physically abused as interrogators demanded to know what he had told his attorneys. Omar's lawyers were never permitted to have him examined to ensure he was healthy and in a good mental state.

It was at this time that Khadr began to turn uncooperative behind bars. He threw urine at guards and took part in a 15-day hunger strike that lasted until he was force-fed and later attacked. In 2005 he refused to eat for 16 days.

Back home in Canada, the news was mixed. The government was taking no action to repatriate Omar and was doing little other than occasional visits to ensure his welfare. His Canadian lawyers, however, were granted an injunction banning CSIS from any further interrogation.

Omar's case was supposed to be heard by a military tribunal. Having been officially deemed an "unlawful enemy combatant" meant no civilian court hearing, but an earlier United States' Supreme Court ruling had affirmed his right to due process. In 2005 Omar was one of 10 prisoners selected for a military tribunal. The prosecutor, however, was replaced three times in 2005 alone.

Omar was ultimately charged with murder by an unprivileged belligerent, attempted murder by an unprivileged belligerent, aiding the enemy and conspiracy with several individuals, including Osama bin Laden and his own father, Ahmed Khadr. The United States did concede to Canada that it would not seek the death penalty for him.

Omar announced to the tribunal that he was going to boycott the hearings because of the inhumane treatment he had received, but the tribunal was quashed before it started hearing evidence, courtesy of a June 29 Supreme Court ruling that the tribunals were unconstitutional.

New legislation was drafted and new charges were sworn against Omar in February 2007, including murder in violation of the law of war, attempted murder in violation of the law of war, conspiracy, providing material support for terrorism and spying. His Canadian attorneys were barred from appearing at his arraignment, but they later decided it was time to start pressuring the Canadian government to bring Omar home.

His legal team eventually won a decisive battle back at home. A federal court judge, having heard the team's case, granted its request for an injunction barring federal agencies such as the Department of Foreign Affairs and International Trade (DFAIT) and CSIS from interrogating Khadr.

"The present case is one of those rare exceptional cases where granting an injunction is required to prevent a potential grave injustice," Judge Konrad von Finckenstein ruled.

The judge ruled that both agencies had violated Omar's Charter rights when, after interviewing him, they turned all of their information over to the United States.

"It's significant that we have a Canadian judge saying that conditions at Guantanamo don't meet Canadian standards," said Dennis Edney, Omar's lawyer in Edmonton.

An election in 2006, however, had brought a change of government with the Conservative Party of Canada unseating the Liberals and winning a minority government. The new Conservative government under Stephen Harper made it quickly known they had no intention of repatriating Khadr. Harper summarized the case, refusing to admit that Omar was a child soldier and stating he had violated American law and that Canada had to respect that process.

Yet by this time, Canada was the only Western country that had not repatriated one of its own citizens detained in Guantanamo Bay. Every other country from Britain to France had been able to bring their citizens back home to face justice. No one was expecting Omar to simply be brought across the border and set free—part of repatriation ensures putting individuals on trial for their actions in their home country or ensuring they serve their sentence at home.

The government's move to keep its evidence against Omar secret took a significant blow in 2007 when Federal Court of Appeal Justice Richard Mosley ordered the government to turn over its records that related specifically to Omar's interrogation, including a videotape of his questioning. In his judgement, Mosley ruled the government had violated international law. The government turned to the Supreme Court of Canada, arguing it was necessary for national security reasons to keep the videotape and evidence secret, but the court did not agree.

On May 23, 2008, the Supreme Court ruled the government had violated the Charter of Rights and Freedoms, specifically Omar's legal rights. The videotapes were released to his lawyers and subsequently ended up in the hands of the media. The faces of CSIS and DFAIT interrogators were obscured, and a skinny, young Omar was clearly visible, asking for fast food and, when left alone, was observed hugging himself and rocking back and forth, crying. The tapes consisted of seven hours of interrogation that took place over four days when he was 16 years old. The two interrogators had used every trick they could think of to get him to talk, offering him cold drinks and oscillating between treating him kindly and sharply.

Specifically, the agents were looking for any information Omar could provide that would help the government locate his father, going so far as telling Omar that his family faced a terrible fate if another government caught them.

"I don't want the Pakistanis to get [Abdullah] because I know how they can treat people," one interrogator stated to Omar at one point.

Omar insisted that he didn't know where his family was. He told his interrogators that he had been left behind at the home of a group of Afghan fighters to serve as a translator, but instead had ended up learning to take apart landmines. He denied any involvement in Speer's death and pleaded that they do something about the torture he was going through. The men accused him of lying, and after four days they simply left.

The revelations triggered a SIRC investigation of CSIS in which the overseeing body lashed out at the agency for failing Omar by refusing to recognize his age as a factor in his treatment and interrogation and that it refused to act on Omar's assertion that he was being tortured.

The argument for repatriating Omar was criticized back at home, not because of the sentiment, but because of the difficulty the case posed. If Canada could persuade the United States to let Omar return home and be put on trial in Canadian court, legal experts concluded that there was very little similar in Canadian law to the charges Omar faced in the United States. Furthermore, much of the evidence had been obtained under "duress" or torture, which meant any of Omar's statements would likely be thrown out of court.

Meanwhile, in the United States, Omar's case was put under intense scrutiny. The government intervened directly by replacing the officer hearing the trial with

another, provoking claims of direct government interference after the first officer made several rulings
against the prosecutors. The evidence against Omar
was cast into doubt—the notes and evidence of soldiers
involved in the firefight led many to question whether
or not Omar had been the one to throw the grenade
that killed Speer. Some troops stated that another militant inside the dwelling had been observed throwing
a grenade several moments before the explosive that
killed Speer was lobbed out of the hut, meaning Omar
hadn't been the only person in the house.

Another soldier had written down his recollection
of the firefight afterwards, and his notes specifically
stated that "the person who threw a grenade that
killed Sgt. 1st Class Christopher J. Speer also died in
the firefight." The wording was later changed to state
that the individual who had thrown the grenade had
been "engaged" in the firefight, not killed.

Meanwhile, Omar's lawyers in Canada were not
finished pressing for the proper treatment of their
client. After a hearing, a federal court judge ruled in
April 2009 that it was obvious Omar's rights had been
violated and that the government was duty bound to
repatriate him at its earliest opportunity. On appeal,
the decision was upheld on a 2–1 vote, the dissenting
vote meaning the government could appeal the case to
the Supreme Court. Canada's highest court decided
to hear the case.

In January 2010, the Supreme Court finally issued
its ruling. The unanimous 9–0 decision stated
Canadian officials had participated in Khadr's

interrogation at Guantanamo Bay, a clear violation of his legal rights. It also concluded he had been treated poorly in order to "soften him up" for interrogation:

> *The deprivation of* [Omar's] *right to liberty and security of the person is not in accordance with the principles of fundamental justice. The interrogation of a youth detained without access to counsel, to elicit statements about serious criminal charges while knowing that the youth had been subjected to sleep deprivation and while knowing that the fruits of the interrogations would be shared with the prosecutors, offends the most basic Canadian standards about the treatment of detained youth suspects.*

However, that was as far as the court went—it did not rule that the government was obligated to return Omar to Canada, leaving that decision up to the Conservatives in power. It was a tricky legal game to play—the government had to weigh the importance of its duty to conduct foreign affairs against its obligation to uphold Omar's rights as granted him under the Canadian Charter of Rights and Freedoms.

In the end, it wasn't a difficult decision for the government to make. On February 16, the Stephen Harper government issued a press release stating it had dispatched a diplomatic note to the United States asking only that the contents of the CSIS interrogation of Omar not be used against him.

Both Omar's lawyers and opposition leaders Michael Ignatieff (Liberal) and Jack Layton (NDP) pounced on the press release, noting that the government still refused to concede that Khadr was, in fact, a child soldier. The note had Omar's lawyers rushing back to court, seeking another injunction to stop the contents of the note from taking effect.

Upon taking office, one of President Barack Obama's first orders was to close down the camps at Guantanamo Bay, but to date, that ruling has not yet taken effect. As of this writing, Omar is still being held at Guantanamo Bay.

CHAPTER ELEVEN

Home-Grown Terror

THE CASE OF OMAR KHADR WAS A real-world example of a trend that CSIS had been fearing and warning the government about for years, dating back to 2005. No longer were the dreaded terrorists restricted to foreigners from across the globe who were trained in deadly arts and then dispatched worldwide to await the signal to execute their pre-arranged plans upon an unsuspecting populace. A new trend was emerging in the fresh-faced recruits who were showing up at terror camps, and CSIS was watching them upon their return home. They were no longer foreigners—they were Canadians.

These potential terrorists were born and bred within Canada into families perhaps once removed from citizenship. They were young, too, and becoming increasingly radicalized, courtesy of their parents who likely harboured anti-Western sympathies, especially given the Allied response in Afghanistan and the invasion of Iraq. An April 2005 report informed Parliament that these children, raised by extremists, were being bred as "prime candidates" for recruitment later in life. What's more, these particular recruits were more adept and potentially deadly than those who had come before.

They were language-savvy—as fluent in English as they were in their native tongue. This new generation was familiar with Western culture—having been raised within an English-speaking society all their lives, these young individuals could easily blend in with the rest of the population, especially in Canada where multiculturalism was not only encouraged but also celebrated as a distinct quality of being Canadian.

More skilled than recruits from other countries—growing up within one of the most technologically advanced nations in the world and being educated in schools where using computers is an everyday part of learning—these new radicals had the technological know-how that they could use in their attacks. They were familiar with Western infrastructure—where government offices were located, where nuclear reactors and other power generating plants were. What's more, these young men and women were learning their radical beliefs at home, courtesy of their parents and extended family. They were the perfect chameleons, able to blend in on the home front and execute their plans without arousing untoward suspicion.

Omar Khadr and his siblings were labelled in a CSIS report as prime examples of this trend, though the Khadrs had been raised both overseas and in Canada. Omar had learned to take apart landmines and build explosives. Two other Khadr sons had become affiliated with terrorist organizations, and yet all were connected to Canada and, for the most part, educated in this country. Omar didn't just read the Koran and play with detonator cord—he also read car magazines.

The 2005 report was never given much public attention because few believed that anyone born and raised in Canada would ever take any violent action against the country. It was a social arrogance soon wiped away when a group of individuals, born and raised in Canada, were rounded up, arrested and put on trial for planning their very own terrorist attack against the country that raised them. And CSIS had been watching all along.

Dubbed "Operation Claymore" by the spy agency, this operation was inspired by an informant within the Muslim community. Mubin Shaikh, 32, a self-described fundamentalist who claimed to be a devout Muslim, had been heavily involved in different agencies of the faith. He was a staunch believer in *sharia*, had helped his sister obtain a Muslim divorce and had lived in Syria between 2002 and 2004. He was a volunteer with a Muslim agency for more than 10 years, was university educated and had served as a cadet in the Canadian Forces.

Shaikh had publicly stated that bombings against Canadian troops overseas were legitimate because the people there were trying to fight off armed soldiers. But he was also known to believe that targeting civilians simply because they are nonbelievers is unacceptable. It was Shaikh's beliefs and the jailing of one his childhood friends after a CSIS investigation that led him into the arms of the agency.

CSIS already knew the terrorist cell existed, consisting mostly of young people, but the agency was running out of options to penetrate the group before something happened. The spy agency had originally tried tactics of diffusion and disruption to stop the youth but was not successful. Shaikh represented CSIS' first real attempt to get someone inside the cell.

After initially interviewing Shaikh, CSIS decided that he would be a valuable asset for infiltrating suspected networks of Canadian terrorists. After a thorough briefing, the agency asked if he would attend a local fundraising banquet scheduled for November 27, 2005, for people being held on security certificates. Shaikh agreed. CSIS gave him photographs to study of individuals it had been watching so that he would recognize them at the fundraiser. The agency urged him to make contact.

"I met with the CSIS guys and they were very interested in me now. So...they put to me the prospect of working for them...," Shaikh later told the CBC's *Fifth Estate*.

Shaikh attended the event and, recognizing several individuals from the photos he had studied, asked them if he could sit down at their table. The alleged leader of the group struck up a conversation with Shaikh, during which the subject of CSIS came up. The man stated to everyone at the table that, if a CSIS agent showed up at his doorstep, he would have no hesitations in shooting him on the spot. In response, Shaikh immediately pulled out his firearms licence and showed it to everyone. In a conversation later that evening, Shaikh was asked if he believed in jihad. The informant responded that he believed holy war was an individual obligation. He passed the leader his contact information and left for home.

Two days later, the group made contact with Shaikh, telling him they were dedicated to creating chaos in Canada and crippling key infrastructure. They asked Shaikh if, based on his military background, he could provide some tactical training to the group. Shaikh agreed, and, between December 18 and 30, he put 18 young men and youths through their paces at a secret camp near Orillia, Ontario. The only weapon the group had was a 9-mm pistol, but every single member got the opportunity to practise shooting it properly. Shaikh supplied the ammunition. The recruits, ranging in age from 15 to 42 years, ran through an obstacle course while being shot at with paintballs. Many of the events at the heavily wooded camp were captured on film, courtesy of the group's leader. On the tape, the leader is heard uttering the words "Rome has to be defeated."

Shaikh later went on to describe himself as the "Godfather" of the group. Because he was the only person with a firearms Possession and Acquisition Licence, he was sent with another group member to buy a gun. He had already paid for 250 rounds of ammunition for the training camp, but Shaikh forked out another $420 for a .22-calibre rifle and 1000 rounds of ammunition. When the two men parted ways, Shaikh immediately handed the gun over to the RCMP, who were now involved in the investigation as well. When questioned by the members of the terrorist cell, Shaikh stated that he had to get rid of the gun because CSIS agents had come to his home to question him.

Shaikh wasn't the only person involved in the investigation—more than 200 police officers were in the area, keeping watch from a discrete distance. The RCMP now dubbed the operation "Project Osage" and were very much involved in monitoring the activities of the group and its members. When Shaikh reported the goals and ambitions of the group to the RCMP and CSIS, they realized they had to act quickly.

According to Shaikh and testimony from one other informant who was involved in the plot, the ultimate goal of the terrorist group was to force Canadian soldiers to withdraw from Afghanistan by mounting terrorist attacks at home. The group had already picked a select array of targets—CSIS headquarters, the broadcasting offices of the CBC, the Toronto Stock Exchange and a military base between Ottawa and Toronto that has not been identified. The more specific plan was to rent U-Haul vans with fake identification, pack them with explosives and detonate them remotely; one co-accused had gone so far as to build and test the detonators that would be used.

The bombings were to take place on three consecutive days, although one member had pressed hard for the attacks to take place on September 11, 2006, so that the date would be remembered forever.

Among the group's most ambitious and sensationalist plans was to storm the Parliament buildings in Ottawa, take the prime minister hostage and behead him. The name of their mission was Operation Badr. The group had also developed a rather interesting fall-back plan in case any of their members were arrested. Those who were still free would attack Toronto police stations with remote control toy cars carrying explosives.

The group was very secretive about its communications: there were no emails and no phone calls. The members specifically chose pagers and computer memory sticks to pass their plans around.

In May 2006, 10 members assembled at the Rockwood Conservation Area for another training mission. The camp was especially important because several members were afraid that the recent arrests of two Americans who were charged with trying to transport handguns across the border could implicate the group—many members of the cell knew both men. Not much training took place at the camp, but plans were beginning to take shape, courtesy of another police informant who had infiltrated the group.

Shaher Elsohemy got involved in the project strictly for the money. He didn't join Project Osage to help his fellow Canadians—he needed cash. The former Air Canada flight attendant was known for his impulsive, expensive spending behaviour, such as making a one-day trip to Poland so he could eat duck properly or taking another one-day trip to South America to eat at his favourite restaurant. He tried to launch his own catering business but instead ended up bankrupt, and an import-export company he started fell through. He then launched both a travel agency and an office for immigration consultation. His need to spend money was greater than his acumen for making it, and he was soon approximately $250,000 in debt.

So when Elsohemy approached CSIS in April 2006 to set up a meeting with the RCMP to help infiltrate the group, cash was the only thing on his mind. His need for money later became a recurring theme throughout the entire trial. When the meeting took place, Elsohemy informed the RCMP that he was willing to help out his country for the tidy sum of $15 million. Six hours of negotiations ensued, with the RCMP talking him down to $13.4 million, a number they still believed was unreasonable. The following day, Elsohemy showed up for a new bargaining session with an itemized list of costs and needs, including:

- $500,000 for loss of revenue

- $400,000 to buy a new house for his parents

- $40,000 to pay off debt

- $125,000 for each of his brothers

The revised total came to $4.5 million, which, after a day of contemplating what Elsohemy could do if they didn't meet his demands, the RCMP returned with an offer of $4.1 million, which included:

- $900,000 for a new house

- $250,000 for his parents

- $40,000 to cover his wife's dental costs

For his part, Elsohemy was given legal immunity from the charge of knowingly facilitating a terrorist activity. He was also asked to help several young people obtain credit cards and purchase ammonium nitrate (a specific kind of fertilizer used to build crude but large bombs) from undercover police officers.

CSIS already knew the group was looking for this substance—a covert entry and search of cell member Zakaria Amara's home turned up business cards for a phony farming company that would be used to cover the purchase.

When Elsohemy had infiltrated the group and earned their trust, Shareef Abdelhaleem gave him $2000 to use as a down payment on a shipment of three tonnes of ammonium nitrate that, as a graduate with an agricultural engineering degree, Elsohemy had convinced the group he could legally purchase.

Ali Imran, 20, was the man whom police stated placed the actual order. The plan was to store the fertilizer at a warehouse in Newmarket. Of course, the substance the police passed on to the terrorists was completely useless.

The undercover operation led to a series of raids on June 2, 2006, that netted 18 suspects, which the media quickly dubbed the "Toronto 18." The arrests and the subsequent charges took the entire country by surprise—the thought that Canadians could be planning a terrorist attack against the country that raised them was almost unthinkable and yet, here it was, happening before their eyes.

The police touched off a bit of a media firestorm when they claimed that the defendants had very little in common; it was later shown that several had attended the same Sunni mosque and that many others had mutual friends.

Intense speculation began regarding just how real the charges were. Fed by denunciations of radical Muslims and a skeptical press, that sentiment was further fuelled when charges against seven of the individuals were stayed for lack of evidence. Only one youth, at that point unidentified under the Youth Criminal Justice Act, was charged, along with 10 adults.

Together, the suspects all faced charges of knowingly participating in a terrorist group, receiving training for enhancing the ability of a terrorist group and intending to cause an explosion of an explosive substance that was likely to cause serious bodily harm or death.

Among those charged were Shareef Abdelhaleem, 30, born in Egypt; Steven Vikash Chand (a.k.a. Abdul Sakur), 25, a former Canadian soldier; Jaamal James, 23, of Toronto; Fahim Ahmad, 21, of Toronto; Asad Ansari, 21, of Mississauga; Zakaria Amara, 20, of Mississauga, Saad Khalid, 19, born in Pakistan; Ali Mohamed Dirie, 26, born in Somalia; Saad Gaya, 22, from Oakville; and Amin Mohamed Durrani, 23, of Toronto.

The Crown shocked the legal community when it announced in June 2007 that it would proceed with a direct indictment, removing the defendants' right to a preliminary hearing to examine the evidence the Crown intended to present in support of the charges. The tactic was specifically aimed at keeping mole Mubin Shaikh off the stand until the last possible moment.

The Crown had good reason to keep their informants off the stand until they absolutely had to bring them forward—both Shaikh and Elsohemy were of questionable backgrounds and with less than patriotic reasons for their participation in the investigation. Shaikh had a past history of illegal drug use, including marijuana, LSD and cocaine. He managed to stay clean for a time but ended up using again in the weeks prior to the arrests of the members of the terrorist cell.

When word of his drug use reached the public, defence attorneys pounced, with Dennis Edney, one of the lawyers for the accused, going so far as to say, "It's essential that the Canadian public is made aware of the extent to which these young men were manipulated and directed by CSIS agents, particularly when one of those agents is an admitted drug addict with a powerful personality."

After the arrests had taken place, with the matter before the courts, Shaikh ended up back in police hands when in April 2007 he was accused of assault and uttering threats against two 12-year-old girls. The girls, it appeared, had ignored Shaikh when he asked them to stop crowding around his children at school one day. The girls allegedly ignored him and yelled racial epithets, at which point Shaikh pushed one of the girls to the ground and said, "I'm going to chop off your legs," before challenging the male students present to a fight. He later pleaded guilty to one count of uttering threats and received a conditional discharge.

Shaikh was also looking for some money. In January 2007 he made it known the RCMP still owed him some $300,000 for his work. In 2008, days before he was scheduled to testify at trial against one of the accused, Shaikh handed a letter to the RCMP demanding $2.4 million in exchange for a pledge to "aggressively defend the evidence and vocally support the role of the agencies involved." The RCMP refused, but Shaikh testified anyway. His behaviour at trial was so erratic that the Crown prosecutor was forced to make the almost unheard-of step of declaring his own witness as hostile so he could confront him with his previous statements and testimony.

In a later interview with *Macleans*, Shaikh stated:

> *I would like to know who in the courtroom is there free of charge. I'm sure the judge is not there because of his love for justice. I'm sure the media isn't there because of the right for public to know. And the lawyers aren't there because they're crusading for justice. Everybody is there for a dollar.*

The motivation of Elsohemy was particularly suspect, but the Crown plowed ahead with its case. The first to crack was one of the youth, Nishanthan Yogakrishnan, found guilty of participating in the terrorist group and conspiring to set off explosives and rush Parliament. Because Yogakrishnan was sentenced as an adult, the publication ban on his name was removed, and he was sentenced to two-and-a-half years in jail, covered by time already served in pre-trial custody. His conviction was the first ever under Canada's 2001 Anti-terrorism Act.

In May 2009, Saad Khalid pleaded guilty to his role in planning to bomb the Toronto Stock Exchange, CSIS headquarters and a military base. He received 14 years in jail. Saad Gaya from Oakville received a sentence of 12 years in prison for his role. Those pleas were followed in September by Ali Mohamed Dirie, a Canadian citizen born in Somalia who demonstrated as little repentance as possible behind bars. In pre-trial custody, Dirie, who had been selected to drive one of the trucks to its intended target, spent his time planning to buy more guns and recruit more inmates into the terrorist group. He struck a corrections officer and on one occasion was recorded calling white people the "number one filthiest people on the face of the planet, they don't even have Islam, they're the most filthiest people," adding later, "In Islam there is no racism, we only hate *kufar* [non-Muslims]."

In October 2009, the leader of the group, Zakaria Amara, now all of 23 years old, pleaded guilty in a Brampton courtroom. In January 2010 he received the stiffest punishment possible under the Anti-terrorism Act—a life sentence.

"I deserve nothing less than your complete contempt," Amara told the court.

On January 20, 2010, Amin Mohamed Durrani pleaded guilty to his involvement in the plot and was sentenced to seven-and-a-half years in prison. The following day, Shareef Abdelhaleem was found guilty of terrorism-related offences, with sentencing to follow at a later date.

The remaining four men are scheduled to go to trial in the spring of 2010.

Although Shaikh later granted interviews about his time as an RCMP informant and reportedly kicked his drug habit again by turning to his faith, Elsohemy was placed in the witness protection for his own safety.

The Toronto 18, by far the most sensational case of home-grown terrorism in Canada to date, was not the only instance of young Canadians ready to take up arms for terrorist causes. Another young Canadian, followed and investigated by CSIS, ended up making headlines for his role in a potential global terrorist plot.

Mohammad Momin Khawaja was born in Canada to parents who immigrated to Canada from Pakistan. Apart from living with his family in Saudi Arabia for five years when he was aged nine to 14, Khawaja grew up in Canada. He graduated from high school in Ottawa and attended Algonquin College, where he graduated from a three-year computer program. He became devoutly religious, teaching youth at a local mosque. In January 2002, he headed to Pakistan for three months to try to find a wife, but CSIS alleges that this trip was for the purpose of obtaining terrorist training, followed by another trip to Pakistan in July 2003 to attend another four-day camp. Any concerns about Khawaja were not initially apparent, because he managed to secure work within the government, first for Human Resources Development Canada as a software engineer and again in 2002 in a similar position on contract to the Department of Foreign Affairs.

Khawaja's interests suddenly broadened. He began making regular appearances at paintball businesses and gun ranges, usually signing in under a pseudonym. Apparently at the request of a friend, Khawaja stored two rifles and some ammunition under his bed at his parents' house. He returned to Pakistan in October 2003 and received several items—including a cell phone and a number of SIM cards—and cash, which he later took to another source inside Pakistan.

It was Khawaja's travels that eventually brought him to the attention of CSIS, the RCMP and numerous other global intelligence officers. On Friday, February 20, 2004, Khawaja flew to London, where he produced a passport with three stamps of entry for Pakistan, proof of having a home residence in Ottawa and his Department of Foreign Affairs identification. After passing through customs, the Canadian met two other individuals who were waiting for him outside the airport—Omar Khyam, 22, and Khyam's brother Shujah Mahmood, 17.

Although Khawaja himself did not attract the attention of the London Metropolitan Police, the two men waiting for him were already under surveillance for alleged terror links to al-Qaeda—along with 50 others suspected of providing aid to the terrorist organization.

There was another twist to the story too—a recent police interview at a London storage unit had turned up a young man who had stored 600 kilograms of ammonium nitrate in his locker. Although he claimed he was using it for a garden, the amount of fertilizer in the storage unit "was enough to cover several soccer pitches."

The London police promptly contacted the RCMP for information on Khawaja, but a background check turned up very little. A request to the National Security Agency (NSA), responsible for signals intelligence in the United States, plucked a conversation out of mid-air using its listening posts and satellites, that originated in Pakistan and connected in Britain. The gist of the message contained instructions on how to make a bomb out of ammonium nitrate. The British recipient of the message was Omar Khyam, who at that very moment was meeting with Khawaja.

MI5, Britain's counter-intelligence agency, had already bugged Khyam's residence. The microphones picked up Khawaja's voice telling Khyam about some kind of detonator.

"So the receiver, what it does basically, gets the signal when you press the button on the transmitter it receives a signal and the output...if you have detonator wires hooked up that will send a charge down the line to whatever you're sending it," the Canadian said at one point.

A surveillance team later followed the group to an Internet café and watched Khawaja showing a group of men images of what appeared to be electronic components.

Back in Canada, the only information CSIS and the RCMP were able to turn up was that Khawaja worked for Foreign Affairs and that he was the registered owner of three semi-automatic rifles. His father was a scholar and academic, but interviews revealed that the family was not terribly religious—only Khawaja had attended mosque in recent years.

Both CSIS and the RCMP were now looking at a global terrorist threat with a home-grown component. With memories of the Maher Arar scandal still fresh in their minds, the group promptly dubbed the operation "Project Awaken" and set to work. But there was now an added sense of urgency. MI5 was reporting conversations recorded from homes belonging to other men linked to Khyam. The conversations contained references to particular targets—critical infrastructure such as gas and electrical utilities, as well as popular nightclubs and shopping centres.

Within one week, an undercover operation in Britain resulted in an inert substance being swapped for the ammonium nitrate in the storage locker. An undercover agent working the front desk at the storage site kept a lookout for Khyam.

In Canada, the RCMP Integrated National Security Enforcement Teams, as well as CSIS, were on the ground trying to learn more about Khawaja. They applied for and were granted warrants for his private communications, bank accounts and computer at the Department of Foreign Affairs. The subsequent haul proved frightening. Several messages between Khyam and Khawaja discussed the development of the "Hi-Fi Digimonster," believed to be a remote-control detonator for explosives. In one email, dated October 19, 2003, Khawaja wrote:

I will start on the remote devices thing right away and will let u [sic] *know once we have it ready for testing and i find some of the things for testing. Urea, nitro phosphate, anything else we need.*

Several other emails related to Khawaja's commitment to jihad, violence and his training in Pakistan and offered plenty of praise for the hijackers responsible for the 9/11 attacks.

Between CSIS, the RCMP and the British and American authorities, there was a growing sense that they had stumbled onto something that was much bigger than it originally appeared.

When Khawaja returned to Canada, CSIS' Physical Surveillance Unit was put in charge of keeping an eye on him at all times. It was not until March 29, 2004, that the authorities finally moved in. With the intelligence side complete, Khawaja was now solely in the hands of the RCMP. A team of police officers stormed his office at the Department of Foreign Affairs while a squad of tactical officers searched his parents' home. Across the ocean, five more individuals were taken into custody within hours of Khawaja's arrest and another two later arrested.

Khawaja was charged with helping to develop bomb detonators, possession of explosives, helping to finance terrorist activity, receiving terrorist training and facilitating terrorism. He became the first person to be charged under the new offences created by the 2001 Anti-terrorism Act.

After electing to have the case heard without a jury, Khawaja was found guilty on all charges by Justice Douglas Rutherford on October 29, 2008.

> *Momin Khawaja was aware of the group's purposes, and whether he considered them terrorism or not, he assisted the group in many ways in the pursuit of its terrorist objectives. It matters not whether any terrorist activity was actually carried out.*

On March 12, 2009, he was sentenced to 10½ years in prison on top of the five years he had already served in pre-trial custody. That sentence fell well short of the two life sentences plus 44 to 58 additional years the Crown had originally been seeking.

On April 14, 2009, the Crown announced that it would appeal the 10½-year sentence imposed by Rutherford, claiming it did not reflect the seriousness of the crimes at hand. The appeal has not yet been ruled on.

CHAPTER TWELVE

Growing Pains

BEYOND ITS WORK COUNTERING potential terrorist attacks at home and abroad—as well as overseeing the security certificate process and the scandal that erupted from the case of Omar Khadr—CSIS has found plenty of other matters to occupy its attention during the last two decades. Some of its activities were quiet, and some were spread publicly across the country as the agency continued to pursue its many responsibilities in protecting the security of Canada.

The number of threats was seemingly ongoing, with many having both terrorism and counter-espionage links. In June 2002, CSIS turned its attention to the growing threat of terrorist groups acquiring radioactive materials not necessarily for building a crude nuclear device but for use in what was dubbed a "dirty bomb."

In essence, such an explosive was a traditional bomb wrapped in damaging radioactive material that, when detonated, spreads the highly dangerous substance across a wide swath. If detonated at ground level, such a bomb could contaminate an area as small as a city block, but the affected area could be as large as thousands of square kilometres if detonated in the air.

The result would be massive panic, CSIS reported, along with the potential contamination of city streets and buildings, as well as vital infrastructure, particularly water resources.

A CSIS report three years earlier had noted that terrorists didn't need to steal from a nuclear processing site to find what it was looking for—radioactive materials were used throughout the medical world, as well as in the oilfield industry. The report cited 200 instances a year in the United States in which radioactive materials from the medical field were reported missing or stolen. That evidence was coupled with plans and materials recovered at safe houses and storage bunkers overrun in Afghanistan, which revealed plans for crude dirty bombs, as well as jars, drums and cases of low-grade uranium.

In addition, espionage by foreign interests was proving to still be an everyday threat in Canada, and CSIS was going as far as it could to weed out potential spies. In 2002, amid a heavy crackdown in China on the spiritual movement of Falun Gong, the agency turned its attention not to believers but to Chinese immigrants in Canada who were still critical of the spiritual group. On many occasions, Falun Gong dissenters were taken aside and asked if they were spies for the Chinese government. The thought was that Chinese Canadians, at the urging of the Chinese government, could be keeping tabs on critics of the regime overseas.

CSIS had good reason to be suspicious. Numerous reports tabled before the cabinet and Parliament had repeatedly cited one country in particular that was the most deeply engaged in spycraft and espionage involving Canadian targets—specifically technological, economic and military information. Although versions of the report released to media agencies had the name of the country redacted, analysts and experts widely believed that country was China.

Operation Sidewinder might have been something of a debacle, but there was a definite sense that China was not only looking for whatever it could get its hands on but was also keeping its eyes on citizens who lived overseas and were critical of the Communist government.

One particular case dating back to the 1990s highlighted this concern. Yong Jie Qu came to Montréal from China in 1991 and enrolled in graduate studies at Concordia University. As soon as classes began, Qu became a fixture in the student community, joining the Chinese Students and Scholars Association (CSSA). In 1994 he applied for permanent resident status and was subsequently interviewed twice by federal visa officers and once by CSIS. His request for residency was later denied based on CSIS' suspicions that he was engaging in acts of espionage and subversion within Canada.

At the time, the Chinese Ministry of State and Security was known to monitor dissident groups overseas, as well as harassing and threatening Chinese students critical of the government. Qu, who was briefly placed under surveillance, was observed regularly reporting to the Chinese embassy in Canada and was seen meeting with a suspected officer of China's

Ministry of State and Security. Interviews with other members of the CSSA turned up suspicions that Qu was trying to persuade the student group to refrain from criticizing the Chinese government.

The case eventually went to court, and although a Federal Court Justice agreed with the evidence CSIS tendered, he ruled that the CSSA was not a government institution or process and, in effect, no actual "spying" had taken place. Citizenship and Immigration appealed the judgement, arguing that the ruling essentially meant that any country could dispatch however many spies it wanted to Canada so long as they weren't actively spying on or trying to subvert any group that was not associated with the government or its processes.

The Chinese government wasn't the only nation with a heavy spy presence inside Canada. The former Cold War giant Russia was still very active in Canada, recruiting agents and planting illegals, as demonstrated in 1995 in the case of Operation Stanley Cup.

CSIS employees and some members of the public got the opportunity to revisit the "good old days" when, in 2002, CSIS put on a display of Cold War spy tools. Obtained mostly between the 1940s and 1960s, the items included a briefcase with a built-in tape recorder, a toy truck with decoding equipment hidden under the hood, a cigarette lighter that contained a wide-angle camera and the five-shot, 8-mm revolver Igor Gouzenko once had in his possession. The items were described as taken from "a foreign intelligence service hostile to Canada" but were clearly Russian in origin.

Other highlights included a hollow AA battery that could be used to store microfilm and a real-looking stick that was not really a stick but a hollowed-out item that spies could roll their information inside of and leave anywhere for their contact to pick up later.

In total, the display contained 750 items, some of which were still considered so secret that some CSIS employees were not allowed to see them, and they were put on display in a secure room. The Communications Security Establishment (CSE) contributed to the exhibit a German Enigma coding machine, a lock-picking kit and a hollowed-out American quarter used to pass along information.

Nostalgia was all well and good, but the Russians were still active in the real, modern world of intelligence, and CSIS was proving—at least publicly—to be effective in tracking down Russia's spies and throwing them out of the country.

In July 2001, Colonel Vladimir Androsov arrived in Ottawa. He had been dispatched to the Russian embassy in Ottawa as the assistant military, naval and air force attaché for the Russian Federation. In reality, Androsov was a spy, a colonel in the military intelligence wing of the Russian armed forces known as the GRU. He had no intentions of being an attaché in the truest sense of the word. He had his orders—he had to somehow get his hands on a Canadian database that his government deemed to be a critical intelligence asset.

In typical fashion, Androsov worked slowly, eventually approaching a Canadian who had access to classified defence-related information. Through the use of cash payments totalling thousands of dollars, Androsov cultivated the man, who was never publicly named, to become his agent. CSIS was watching the entire time, finding Androsov's repeated meetings with the same individual curious.

Despite the colonel's best efforts to make his days seem as uninteresting as possible, he was observed to be engaging in such tactics as taking long drives to pointless destinations or using circuitous routes to meet with his new agent in an effort to shake whatever tail might be following him at the time.

In October 2002, after sufficient time had passed, Androsov finally made his move, asking his agent to get the disc containing the database for him. The material contained in the database was of classified military technology. Upon learning of this request, CSIS launched into more direct action. It got in touch with the Department of Foreign Affairs, which subsequently asked the Russian government to recall Androsov from Canada. Russia did, but as is typical in the world of international diplomacy and espionage, it expelled a few Canadian diplomats from the embassy in Russia in turn.

Because CSIS sought to keep the entire affair under wraps, the Canadian agent was never charged. He wasn't even fired. He was simply moved to a job where he did not have access to sensitive or classified information.

About five years later, CSIS scored another victory in the espionage war against Russia, only this time it was much more public, and it was celebrated as a win by the agency itself.

On November 16, 2006, word trickled out that someone had recently been arrested at Pierre Elliott Trudeau International Airport in Montréal. CSIS alleged that the man arrested, who was using the name Paul William Hampel, was a Russian spy. He had been taken into custody at approximately 6:00 PM on November 14 trying to board a flight out of Canada. The following day, cabinet ministers Stockwell Day and Monte Solberg signed off on a security certificate, accusing Hampel of "engaging in espionage and being a member of an organization engaged in espionage."

The certificate represented the first such document ever issued by the Stephen Harper government, which had won with a minority in a general election earlier that year. The certificate was the first issued since Adil Charkaoui had been arrested in 2003.

The biggest problem facing CSIS, however, was trying to identify who exactly Paul William Hampel really was. His tactics were reminiscent of those of the Sluzhba Vneshney Razvedki (SVR), the Russian government's foreign intelligence agency. "Directorate S" of the SVR was traditionally responsible for planting Russian agents with established "legends," or fraudulent backgrounds, as illegals inside foreign countries— as had had been investigated with Operation Stanley Cup. Legends were traditionally supplied by "Line N" officers who worked at diplomatic postings in the target nation.

An investigation revealed that the man known as Paul William Hampel had slipped into Canada about a decade earlier in order to start building his legend. His arrest had been triggered when he attempted to travel using fake ID. Unlike the two illegals under observation in Operation Stanley Cup—who had used the identities of Canadians who had died as children—he had stolen the identity of a living Canadian.

The Russian embassy in Canada refused to comment on the case, leaving officials at CSIS pretty sure of what they had but no real name to pin on "Hampel." The spy was immediately trotted out before Justice Pierre Blais, who was selected to hear the case asking for his deportation back to Russia.

The evidence tendered with the court revealed that Hampel had been spying on Canada for more than a decade. From his base in Montréal, he had been operating an offshore company, often travelling overseas, usually to the Balkans. He was using a fraudulently acquired birth certificate bearing the name of a real Canadian that he had obtained with a passport in 1995. The passport had been subsequently renewed in 2000 and 2002. At the time of his arrest, his luggage contained $7800 in five different currencies, several bank and credit cards, five cell phone identification cards, two digital cameras and a shortwave radio.

But the most interesting find was a bundle of index cards or "cheat sheets" on Canadian history, politicians, important figures and culture. The crib notes contained information on historical figures such as Jacques Cartier, Samuel de Champlain, various Québec premiers and Canada's prime ministers. There were notes on important institutions and events in Canadian history, such as the Hudson's Bay Company, the Seven Years' War, the Québec Act, the Upper and Lower Canada rebellions of the late early 1800s, the Charlottetown Accords, both world wars and the October Crisis.

When reached for comment, Alexander Kouzminov, a former Directorate S officer for the SVR, went so far as to confirm that "Canada is an attractive country for the SVR."

When Hampel's lawyer complained to Justice Blais about his client's treatment, CSIS sought to justify its methods. Hampel apparently had to eat off the floor while in custody, but that was so he could not be presented with any kind of weapon with which to escape. He was not allowed to flush the toilet in his cell by himself, in case he was trying to get rid of anything he might have hidden inside his body cavities.

Hampel, however, refused to admit that he was a Russian spy, forcing the government to bring out witnesses to support its claims. Dale Hopkins, an investigator for Ontario's Office of the Registrar General, testified before the court that the birth certificate issued to Hampel was a forgery. While there was an actual Canadian by that name, no record existed of a Paul Hampel born in Ontario between 1960 and 1970, casting serious doubt on the spy's alleged birthday of December 11, 1965. Hopkins confirmed that another person by the same name was very much alive in Canada.

"[Mr. Hampel] does not exist," Hopkins told the court. In a moment of levity, Blais suggested maybe the defendant's parents should testify, to which Hampel responded by laughing, something the judge took note of.

Unwilling to go through the entire court process, Hampel finally owned up. On December 5, 2006, he informed the court that he was indeed Russian, although he never confessed to being a spy. His true identity was ordered sealed by Blais.

"My client admits that he is not Paul William Hampel, that he is a Russian citizen, born on October 21, 1961, and that he has no legal status in Canada," Stephane Handfeld, the man's lawyer told the court. With this admission, Justice Blais ordered the "Russian citizen" deported. On December 27, 2006, Hampel boarded a plane for Russia and was sent back home.

Subsequent investigations by the press revealed there was more to "Hampel" than had been revealed in court. He had originally worked in Canada at low-wage jobs, including patrolling pool sides as a lifeguard in order to better establish his legend. He received his first passport in 1995. In 1997, he launched Emerging Markets Research, subsequently registered in Ireland, with assets of $2.3 million.

Besides living in Canada, he had lived in Belgrade, Serbia for two years between 2001 and 2003 where he worked as an amateur photographer, taking pictures of the Serbian landscape that were often published in local newspapers. He self-published a coffee-table book of his own photos. Despite his repeated travels and extended stays in the Balkans, no record existed of him ever doing any kind of business—all he did was take pictures, it appeared.

However, it became apparent that many of his trips to the former Yugoslavia and his travels within the area coincided with major incidents taking place there at the time—he was in Serbia when restless crowds, disputing the results of the September 24, 2000, elections, formed a massive street protest that led to Milosevic's overthrow and departure from Serbia.

Hampel was in Skopje, Macedonia, when ethnic members of the Albanian National Liberation Army militant group attacked the security forces of the Republic of Macedonia in 2001, and he made a visit to Montenegro during the 2006 drive for independence of the republic from its union with Serbia.

CSIS later revealed that it had been tipped off about Hampel's true presence in Canada but would not say how. Speculation put the source of the tip as an informant who had volunteered the information. The arrest, made by agents of the Canada Border Services Agency (CBSA), took place five days before it was publicly announced. For CSIS, it was a counter-intelligence coup as well as a public relations boon that demonstrated its capability in finding foreign spies and having them deported from the country.

In a different area, the government and CSIS were finally starting to make some headway against another common problem in Canada—suspected terrorist financing. The Anti-terrorism Act was designed to finally give the government the means with which to seize the assets of known supporters of terrorist groups, but it took some time before it could be enacted.

In January 2002, the Supreme Court of Canada upheld those laws, declaring that anyone living and working in Canada to support terrorism abroad can be classified as a threat to national security. At issue was the case of Manickavasagam Suresh of the LTTE (Tamil Tigers), who had been fighting deportation to Syria. He was accused of being a "bagman" for the Tigers, funnelling money from Canada back to Sri Lanka to help finance the civil war there. In his case, the court ruled that an individual does not need to be a direct threat to Canada for the person to be labelled a threat to national security. Membership in an organization was not sufficient grounds for this label, but actively supporting any terrorist group put Canada at risk.

"It may once have made sense to suggest that terrorism in one country did not necessarily implicate other countries. But after the year 2001, that approach is no longer valid," the court wrote, dismissing Suresh's claims that his actions were protected by his Charter rights to free speech, expression and association. The court upheld that Suresh could still be deported even if he feared mistreatment in his destination country, so long as he received a fair chance to make his case.

CSIS was still building its case against other terrorist groups with a presence in Canada. Number one on its radar was Hezbollah, a Lebanese-based terrorist group fighting Israel's occupation of parts of Lebanon. CSIS repeatedly alleged that the group was laundering tens of thousands of dollars that were used to buy equipment such as night-vision goggles, blasting caps, computers and cameras to record attacks overseas.

The group in Canada was stealing luxury vehicles and either selling them here for cash or shipping them overseas. Through phone taps, CSIS learned the Hezbollah leadership in Lebanon would contact its followers in Canada with a "shopping list" of items that would then be purchased and shipped overseas.

In December 2002, the government finally took action, outlawing the activities of Hezbollah in Canada, as well those of the Kurdistan Workers' Party (PKK), which is fighting in countries in the Middle East for a homeland for the Kurdish people, and of Aum Shinrikyo, the Japanese cult responsible for the fatal March 20, 1995, sarin nerve gas attack on the Japanese transit system. All of their assets were frozen, and the banks were told to check their records for holdings by any of the groups and to contact CSIS if they found any.

Added earlier that year to the "listed entities" known to be involved with terrorism were such groups as al-Qaeda, al-Jihad, Groupe Islamique Armé and Hamas, a violent group fighting in the Palestinian territories against Israel, as well as five groups in Canada linked to it.

In May 2005, Mujahedin-e Khalq (MEK), an Iranian terrorist group dedicated to the overthrow of the current Iranian regime, was outlawed, as was Kahane Chai, a right-wing Jewish terrorist organization dedicated to expanding the boundaries of Israel.

CANADIAN SECURITY INTELLIGENCE SERVICE

In total, the list at the time contained some 35 groups (as of April 2010, it has 42 names). The penalty for supporting any of them was 10 years in jail.

Fundraising for terrorism continued to involve large sums of money, though. Canada's Financial Transactions and Reports Analysis Centre (FINTRAC) announced in 2005 that it had tagged nearly $180 million in suspected terrorist financing in 2004, all of which was forwarded to CSIS and the RCMP.

In April 2006, the Stephen Harper Conservative government, based on repeated reports from CSIS, finally did what the Liberals had openly refused to do—they outlawed LTTE and the many different wings associated with it while doing their best to avoid interfering with legitimate non-profit organizations.

On the home front, it seemed that CSIS was doing rather well. But a string of public incidents involving some of its personnel were increasingly attracting more attention. In April 2003 Theresa Sullivan, a 12-year veteran of CSIS, was dismissed for having a secret relationship with an "operational person of interest," meaning the individual was suspected of being either a spy or a terrorist. The man, identified only as "A.B." had first met Sullivan, who was married at the time, in December 1996, and the pair got together several more times. In February 1998, Sullivan returned to her home to find the house empty and her husband gone—he had left her.

Although she had not told A.B. about her husband's departure, A.B. seemed to know and called her repeatedly, and he sent her jewellery, which she showed off at work. The CSIS brass grew concerned and ordered her to stop contact with the man. She ignored the order, travelling to see the man in 1999 without informing CSIS first. Shortly afterward, A.B. stopped calling, but he then made contact again in February 2000. Eventually, Sullivan told him to stop calling her, but it was too late. Following an investigation, her security clearance was removed for disobeying an order; without it, she could no longer work for CSIS.

In its work, CSIS has faced criticisms of wrongdoing from individuals within the communities they were targeting. In July 2005, the agency made the rare move to go public with an accusation made against it. A woman of Muslim faith had apparently confided in her imam that two agents had come to her Scarborough apartment looking for her husband, who was suspected of terrorist involvement. When he wasn't there, it was alleged, they verbally assaulted her, then pushed her to the floor.

The allegations were made by Aly Hindy, the woman's imam at the Salaheddin Islamic Centre, who then circulated a pamphlet containing the woman's claims. According to the pamphlet, the two agents called her a "bitch" and told her, "Now we're going to show you what rights we have," before assaulting her.

"CSIS really takes umbrage with these allegations," spokesperson Kathryn Locke told the media. Hindy was no stranger to CSIS. Ahmed Khadr had worshipped at his mosque, and Hindy had been the only imam of a group in Canada that refused to sign a letter condemning the London bombings. CSIS had previously interviewed Hindy's son, who had travelled with the Khadrs in Pakistan in 2000.

In the end, the accusations amounted to nothing. Despite an internal investigation and an outside investigation conducted by Toronto police, there was no evidence that such an incident ever occurred. After a four-month probe, neither the agency nor the police force ever learned the identity of the woman who was said to have made the allegations, and CSIS had never been able to interview anyone with knowledge of them. Hindy had refused to tell the police who she was.

"In the absence of co-operation, it's impossible to complete an investigation," said Toronto Police Service spokesperson Mark Pugash.

There was another concern growing within CSIS, but it had little to do with the agency itself. Scores of young Canadian men with roots in Somalia were starting to disappear. During the later part of the first decade of the 21st century, Somalia had become one of the most turbulent countries in the world. A civil war was raging between a militant Islamist group—the Supreme Council of Islamic Courts—and the legitimate government, so much so that the government had to rely on Ethiopian troops to beat the militants back. Ayman al-Zawahiri, a prominent leader of al-Qaeda, had called for all followers to join the militants to fight in Somalia, and it appeared that men from all over the world were responding, especially individuals from Canada.

Although only 28 Canadians are registered with the Department of Foreign Affairs as being in Somalia, CSIS estimated the actual number to be between 1000 and 5000 people. CSIS' fears were punctuated by reports of Canadian passports and identification being found on dead bodies in Somalia. In November 2009, a Toronto mosque asked for information to track down six members they feared were fighting in Somalia. CSIS was involved, as well as the RCMP, because 20 men from Minneapolis in the United States had turned up in Somalia fighting for a terrorist group. Eight men, in turn, had been charged with recruiting some of the 20 men and paying for their airfare and weapons. Several died.

One Canadian allegedly called home from Kenya after leaving for Somalia, but he has not been heard from since. Groups have been releasing English-language propaganda in Somali communities within Canada that encourage Western Somali youth to take up the battle. CSIS' concerns are twofold—first, that young men are being recruited and shipped overseas to be trained as terrorists where they could possibly be killed, and second, that, if they return home, they will do so as hardened veterans and seasoned terror-ists who could pose a risk to the security of Canada.

Ultimately it is difficult for CSIS to gauge activity in foreign countries because it is not tasked with con-ducting foreign intelligence. It has more than 200 agreements with various agencies in other countries allowing CSIS agents to operate there, specifically to investigate potential threats to Canada that originate in other nations, but those agents perform no intelligence-gathering role on foreign governments.

Since the late 1990s, the different governments have bounced the idea of a Canadian foreign intelligence service back and forth but have never been able to settle on whether or not they want to set one up, and if they do, whether it will become a responsibility of CSIS or its own separate agency.

At the moment, CSIS receives the bulk of its foreign intelligence from information-sharing arrangements with the United States, Great Britain and Australia, but it has been routinely criticized, both at home and abroad, for its lack of an international presence. The constant theme of the criticism is that if Canada wants to be a major global player, it has to get its hands dirty in the world of foreign intelligence. Only time will tell if the Canadian government will ever take that step.

Notes on Sources

Alberts, Sheldon. "CSIS sends spies on overseas missions." *National Post*, October 19, 2001.

Arnold, Tom. "Stop your killing or be killed." *National Post*, January 22, 2000.

Barrett, Tom. "Judge orders CSIS to stop interrogating Khadr." *National Post*, August 10, 2005.

Bell, Stewart: "Ahmed Khadr provided references for would-be terrorists: Judge." *National Post*, December 31, 2009.

—— "Alleged spy in Canadian agents' sights for a while, Day hints." *National Post*, November 29, 2006.

—— "Al-Qaeda's Canadian vanguard." *National Post*, September 6, 2002.

—— "Banks ordered to freeze assets linked to Hamas." *National Post*, September 16, 2003.

—— "Canadian hunger striker being force-fed in U.S. prison." *National Post*, June 10, 2009.

—— "Canadian terrorist gets life." *National Post*, January 19, 2008.

—— "Case tainted, terror suspect's lawyer argues." *National Post*, July 3, 2009.

—— "CSIS defends secrecy in terrorism case." *National Post*, January 17, 2001.

—— "CSIS displays gadgets from Cold War spies." *National Post*, September 28, 2002.

—— "CSIS links Toronto teacher to Jihad." *National Post*, August 28, 2001.

—— "CSIS was worried lost sensitive papers could end up in wrong hands." *National Post*, February 4, 2000.

—— "CSIS watched Ressam for years before arrest." *National Post*, April 7, 2001.

—— "Egyptian key man in terror group: CSIS." *National Post*, March 26, 2009.

—— "FBI's Canadian songbird." *National Post*, May 3, 2007.

—— "Gone, feared enlisted; A Toronto Imam worries his young, 'emotional' followers are being targeted for jihad." *National Post*, December 12, 2009.

—— "Groups act as fronts for terror: CSIS." *National Post*, December 9, 2000.

—— "Hezbollah uses Canada as base: CSIS." *National Post*, October 31, 2002.

—— "How to identify terrorist activity: The official guide." *National Post*, May 24, 2006.

—— "Jihadists born here pose new threat." *National Post*, November 19, 2005.

—— "Khadr killed in gunfight: Report." *National Post*, October 14, 2003.

—— "Mosque seeks Somali youth." *National Post*, November 26, 2009.

—— "No charges as police close probe into imam's claims." *National Post*, December 9, 2005.

—— "Refugee held after CSIS probe." *National Post*, December 13, 2002.

—— "Return of the spying game." *National Post*, June 7, 2007.

—— "Ruling will help Canada eject terrorists." *National Post*, January 12, 2002.

—— "Russia quiet on alleged spy arrest." *National Post*, November 17, 2006.

—— "Somali-Canadians joined fight in Horn of Africa." *National Post*, July 26, 2007.

—— "Some Canadians tried to join Taliban." *National Post*, March 27, 2002.

—— "The spy who loved him and then lost her job." *National Post*, April 23, 2003.

—— "Sri Lanka's civil war and the Canadian connection." *National Post*, June 3, 2000.

—— "Tamil Tigers supporters 'not welcome.'" *National Post*, April 11, 2006.

—— "Terror fundraising hits $180M." *National Post*, November 5, 2005.

—— "Terror report blames CSIS." *National Post*, October 30, 2007.

—— "Terrorists are using Canada as staging ground: CSIS." *National Post*, May 3, 2000.

—— "Toronto 18 terrorist jailed seven years." *National Post*, October 3, 2009.

—— "Toronto man linked to bin Laden should be deported: Judge." *National Post*, October 6, 2001.

—— "Unidentified country spying on Canada." *National Post*, January 3, 2001.

Bell, Stewart and Adrian Humphreys. "'A gold mine' for spy agency." *National Post*, December 27, 2006.

—— "Alleged spy says he's Russian." *National Post*, December 5, 2006.

—— "'He's a ghost': Trail of Russian 'spy' winds from Serbia to Montreal to Cyprus." *National Post*, November 22, 2006.

—— "Ottawa girds for diplomatic fallout: Russian deported." *National Post*, December 27, 2009.

—— "Suspected spy arrested: False identity a Russian technique." *National Post*, November 16, 2006.

Bell, Stewart and Katie Rook. "Man tells CBC he's terror mole." *National Post*, July 14, 2006.

Bell, Stewart and Marina Jimenez. "Al-Qaeda operatives in Canada." *National Post*, December 15, 2001.

Blackwell, Tom. "Man accused of bin Laden ties will likely be deported." *National Post*, November 20, 2001.

—— "Public servants face criminal charges under secrets law." *National Post*, April 3, 2002.

Blanchfield, Mike. "Ottawa allows man to return." *National Post*, June 19, 2009.

Boer, Peter. *Canadian Spies and Spies in Canada: Undercover at Home and Abroad.* Edmonton, AB: Folklore Publishing, 2005.

Bolan, Kim. "Air India warning had right date; Told to mind his own business, official testifies." *National Post*, May 4, 2007.

Bolan, Kim. "Bartleman testimony rejected; Air India Inquiry." *National Post*, December 7, 2007.

—— *Loss of Faith: How the Air-India Bombers Got Away with Murder.* Toronto, ON: McClelland and Stewart, 2005.

Bronskill, Jim. "Protests over modified crops to escalate: CSIS." *National Post*, February 12, 2001.

—— "Rumours, not fact, scuttled Chinese spy report: CSIS." *National Post*, April 25, 2000.

—— "'Welcome mat' for spies feard." *National Post*, May 21, 2001.

Cherry, Paul. "Judge scoles spying suspect's lawyers for being unprepared." *National Post*, November 29, 2006.

Cleroux, Richard. *Official Secrets: The Inside Story of the Canadian Security Intelligence Service.* Toronto, ON: McClelland and Stewart, 1991.

Cobb, Chris. "More terrorism charges for Canadian man: Momin Khawaja." *National Post*, December 21, 2005.

Cowan, James. "No easy options in Khadr case, experts warn." *National Post*, July 17, 2008.

D'Andrea, Armando. "CSIS urges no release for terror suspect." *National Post*, July 20, 2005.

Dawson, Fabian. "RCMP report on Chinese influence altered by CSIS." *National Post*, February 23, 2000.

Dion, Robert. *The Crimes of the Secret Police.* Montréal, QC: Black Rose Books, 1982.

Dube, Francine. "Arars sue Canada for $400M in damages." *National Post*, April 22, 2004.

Duffy, Andrew. "Al-Qaeda banker links alleged." *National Post*, November 5, 2008.

—— "CSIS testimony in doubt; Spy agency ordered to turn over file on Harkat." *National Post*, May 28, 2009.

—— "Harkat once worked for Khadr, CSIS alleges." *National Post*, May 30, 2009.

—— "Informant in Harkat case failed lie detector." *National Post*, June 6, 2009.

—— "Judge orders CSIS to open secret file in Harkat case." *National Post*, October 21, 2009.

—— "Terror suspect released again from Kingston jail." *National Post*, December 1, 2009.

—— "U.S. judge blasts CSIS in Ressam trial." *National Post*, March 28, 2001.

Eby, Chris. "Store clerk denies link to bin Laden." *National Post*, February 27, 2001.

Edwards, Stevens. "Watchdog raps CSIS of Khadr." *National Post*, July 16, 2009.

Farnsworth, Clyde. "Canada's Security Agency accused of spying on Canadians." *New York Times*, August 28, 1994.

Fife, Robert. "China spying on us." *National Post*, December 29, 2004.

—— "CSIS says it has thick file on Khawaja." *National Post*, April 2, 2004.

—— "PM to House: Move fast on terror bill." *National Post*, October 16, 2001.

Fife, Robert and Stewart Bell. "U.S. let CSIS, RCMP question Khadr." *National Post*, December 27, 2002.

Goodspeed, Peter. "Dirty bombs 'credible threat,' experts warn." *National Post*, June 11, 2002.

Gordon, James. "Arar hopes for vindication and a return to 'normal' life." *National Post*, September 16, 2006.

Gordon, Sean. "Federal officials gagging inquire, Maher Arar charges." *National Post*, December 21, 2004.

Hamilton, Dwight. *Inside Canadian Intelligence: Exposing the New Realities of Espionage and the International Terrorism*. Toronto, ON: Dundrun Press, 2006.

Hamilton, Graeme. "Canadian's return blocked by UN." *National Post*, April 11, 2009.

—— "Case against terror suspect formally halted." *National Post*, October 15, 2009.

—— "Charkaoui a free man; All restrictions lifted." *National Post*, September 25, 2009.

—— "Charkaoui told CSIS about jihad recruiting." *National Post*, January 23, 2008.

—— "Court eases bail terms for alleged sleeper agent." *National Post*, February 21, 2009.

Jiwa, Salim and Donald J. Hauka. *Margin of Terror: A Reporter's Twenty-Year Odyssey Covering the Tragedies of the Air India Bombing*. Toronto, ON: Key Porter Books, 2006.

Kari, Shannon. "Khadr 'looked healthy,' CSIS agent testifies." *National Post*, October 16, 2009.

Laidlaw, Katherine. "Details of alleged bomb plot revealed." *National Post*, June 23, 2009.

Leong, Melissa. "Mole heard of terror plans, court hears." *National Post*, June 11, 2008.

Mitrovica, Andrew. *Covert Entry: Spies, Lies and Crimes Inside Canada's Secret Service*. Toronto, ON: Random House, 2002.

—— "Front man." *The Walrus*, September 2004.

O'Toole, Megan. "Becoming a police agent my duty, witness says; Toronto 18." *National Post*, January 16, 2010.

Security Intelligence and Review Committee. *The Heritage Front Affair*. 1995.

Simons, Paula and Jodie Sinnema. "Khadr claims no choice but to fight; CSIS interview." *National Post*, July 16, 2008.

Tibbetts, Janice. "Canada complicit in Khadr prosecution, top court rules." *National Post*, May 24, 2008.

—— "Judge ends surveillance of ex-terror suspect." *National Post*, December 18, 2009.

—— "Terror suspect can say, court rules." *National Post*, December 15, 2009.

Tibbetts, Janice and Jan Ravensberg. "CSIS wrong to destroy evidence, court says." *National Post*, July 27, 2008.

Vincent, Isabel. "CSIS makes rare public defence of its actions." *National Post*, July 27, 2005.

Peter Boer

Peter Boer is an author and journalist based in St. Albert and is a co-editor for the *St. Albert Gazette* newspaper. He has a degree in psychology from the University of Alberta in Edmonton and a graduate diploma in journalism from Concordia University in Montréal. He has 10 other books to his credit, including *Bush Pilots: Canada's Wilderness Daredevils, Canadian Spies and Spies in Canada* and *Canadian Crime Investigations: Hunting Down Serial Killers* for Folklore Publishing.